Dynamite Cover Letters

Books and CD-ROMs by Drs. Ron and Caryl Krannich

DYNAMITE COVER LETTERS

AND OTHER GREAT JOB SEARCH LETTERS

Fourth Edition

Ronald L. Krannich, Ph.D.
Caryl Rae Krannich, Ph.D.

IMPACT PUBLICATIONS
Manassas Park, VA

DYNAMITE COVER LETTERS AND OTHER GREAT JOB SEARCH LETTERS

Fourth Edition

Library of Congress Cataloging-in-Publication Data

Krannich, Ronald L.
    Dynamite cover letters and other great job search letters / Ronald L.
  Krannich,
  Caryl Rae Krannich.—4th. ed.
      p. cm.
  Includes bibliographical references and index.
  ISBN 1-57023-101-X
    1. Job hunting 2. Cover letters. I. Krannich, Caryl Rae. II. Title.
HF5382.7.K693   1999
650.14—dc20
                                            98-46204
                                                CIP

Publisher: For information on Impact Publications, including current and forthcoming publications, authors, press kits, online bookstore, and submission requirements, visit Impact's Web site: *www.impactpublications.com*

Publicity/Rights: For information on publicity, author interviews, and subsidiary rights, contact the Public Relations Department: Tel. 703/361-7300.

Sales/Distribution: All bookstore sales are handled through Impact's trade distributor: National Book Network, 15200 NBN Way, Blue Ridge Summit, PA 17214, Tel. 1-800-462-6420. All other sales and distribution inquiries should be directed to the publisher: Sales Department, IMPACT PUBLICATIONS, 9104-N Manassas Drive, Manassas Park, VA 20111-5211, Tel. 703/361-7300, Fax 703/335-9486, or Email *cover@impactpublications.com*

Contents

PREFACE ix

CHAPTER 1: The Power and Promise of Paper 1

- Become Powerful   1
- You Are What You Write   2
- Your Writing Skills Do Count   3
- Let's See Your Paper   4
- Improve Your Effectiveness   7
- Get Taken Seriously By Employers   9
- The Product and The Process   10
- Do What's Expected and Produces Results   11
- Choose the Right Resources   13
- Discover Your Paper Power   14

CHAPTER 2: Myths and Realities 16

- The Job Search   16
- Cover Letters   21

CHAPTER 3: Job Search Letters 31

- Cover Letters 31
- Approach Letters 38
- Thank-You Letters 44
- Resume Letters 50
- 13 Examples 51

CHAPTER 4: Form, Structure, and Design 64

- Effective Communication 64
- Form and Structure 66
  - Heading 68
  - Date Line 68
  - Inside Address 69
  - Salutation 70
  - Body and Continuation Pages 72
  - Closing 73
  - Signature Line 74
  - Identification Initials 75
  - Enclosures 76
  - Copy Reference 76
  - Using Postscripts (P.S.) 76
- Typing Styles 77
- Layout and Design 78
- Evaluation 78

CHAPTER 5: Organization and Content 82

- Common Mistakes 82
- Principles of Good Advertising 85
- Planning and Organizing 87
- Content Rules 88
- Inclusions and Omissions 92
- Evaluation 94

CHAPTER 6: Top Quality Production 96

- Production Equipment 96
- Type Style and Size 98
- Justification, Hyphens, Paragraphs 99
- Paper Choices 99
- Produce a "10" Letter 99

CHAPTER 7: Effective Distribution 101

- Distribution Choices and Etiquette 101
- The Envelope 102
- To Whom It May Concern 103
- Best Methods 104
- Targeting 105
- Broadcasting and Junk Mail 106
- Following-Up With Impact 106
- Evaluating 107

CHAPTER 8: Dynamite Implementation & Follow-Up Techniques 109

- From Advice to Action 109
- Implementation for Results 110
- Commit Yourself in Writing 110
- The Art of Follow-Up 112
- How to Kill a Perfect Letter 112
- Rescuing Your Letter 114
- Effective Follow-Up Options 116
- Multiple Follow-Ups 117
- Follow-Up Your Follow-Up 120
- Follow-Up Really Means Following-Up 120
- Evaluate Your Follow-Up Competencies 121

CHAPTER 9: Evaluate Your Effectiveness 123

- Conduct Two Evaluations   123
- Internal Evaluation   124
  – Audience   124
  – Form, Structure, and Design   124
  – Organization and Content   125
  – Production Quality   126
  – Distribution   127
  – Follow-Up Action   127
- External Evaluation   128

CHAPTER 10: The Letter Sampler: 38 Dynamite Examples 130

- Starting a Job Search   132
- Laying the Ground Work   138
- Developing Contacts and Job Leads   142
- Responding to Vacancy Announcements   145
- Cover Letters   156
- Resume Letters   160
- Follow-Up Letters   163
- Thank-You Letters   166

CHAPTER 11: Using Faxes, E-Mail, and the Internet 170

- Faxes   170
- E-Mail   172
- Faxes Versus E-Mail   173
- Major Web Sites   174
- Key Electronic Job Search Resources   176
- Write It Right   177

THE AUTHORS 178

INDEX 180

Preface

Getting strangers to take you seriously is what the job search is all about. You want them to recognize your interests, skills, and qualifications by taking actions that lead to interviews and job offers. In every job search activity—be it writing résumés, telephoning for job leads, networking, or interviewing for a job—you must repeatedly make good first impressions that motivate employers to invest more time in your candidacy. You can make powerful impressions by producing and distributing several types of job search letters that motivate the employer to take action. That's the subject of this book.

Few people practice the art of good letter writing. Indeed, many job seekers put their worst foot forward when writing cover letters. They forget it's their cover letter—not their résumé—that gets read first by employers. Considering letters as relatively unimportant in comparison to other job search activities, they often generate dull, boring, and deadly documents that do anything but grab the attention of readers and persuade them to invest more time with them on the telephone or in a face-to-face interview. In many cases, their letters kill both their résumé and their candidacy. This should not happen to you.

This book is all about paper power—getting it, building it, and using it. It's designed to put more power into your paper and greater energy, enthusiasm, and interpersonal values into your job search. It shows you how to create your own dynamite letters that will lead to greater job search success.

As you will quickly discover, this is not your typical book on cover letters. Most such books are primarily filled with scattered writing tips or examples of so-called "outstanding" letters. Our focus is on both **understanding and action** centered around an important **process** aimed at getting employers to **respond to you in positive ways**.

We begin with the role of cover letters in the overall job search process and then focus on the key principles for creating effective cover letters. We do so by examining every stage of the letter writing process, from organizing and writing internal letter elements to producing, distributing, and following-up each letter for maximum impact. Self-evaluation plays an important role throughout this process.

> **In a job search the power of paper depends on how well you distribute and follow-up your written communications.**

Effective letters involve much more than demonstrating good writing style on attractive paper. At the very least, your letters must be intelligently produced and distributed in reference to the specific needs of your audience. Most important of all, they must be followed-up with the critical telephone call. Neglect any one of these letter writing stages and you will effectively kill your chances of moving employers to respond to you in positive ways. You will produce paper, but your paper will lack power.

In this new edition, we further address the role of electronic communications in the job search, especially the increasing use of faxes, e-mail, and the Internet in lieu of mailing letters and conducting a conventional job search (Chapter 11). Job seekers increasingly must learn how to communicate their qualifications to employers through these electronic mediums. Job seekers who also include faxes, e-mail, and the Internet in their repertoire of job search communication often have an advantage over those who only communicate by mail and telephone. In certain employment situations, job seekers using faxes, e-mail, and the Internet tend to communicate a different level of competence to employers. At the same time, you should not confuse the medium with the message. The structure and content of your message should be consistent, regardless of your method of distribution or transmission.

We wish you well as you initiate your first contacts with potential employers and other individuals for job information, advice, and referrals. Whatever you do, make sure your paper has power—persuades others to take actions favorable to your job search. If you correctly organize, produce, distribute, and follow-up your letters, you will acquire the power to move yourself into the offices of employers.

Whatever you do, make sure you go beyond just writing good or outstanding job search letters. As you will quickly discover, in a job search, the power of paper depends on how well you distribute and follow-up your written communications.

Ronald L. Krannich
Caryl Rae Krannich

Dynamite Cover Letters

1

The Power and Promise of Paper

We know résumés play a key role in the job search process. Whether in paper or electronic formats, they are one of the most efficient and effective mediums for establishing communications between candidates and employers. They provide job seekers with an opportunity to present their key qualifications to employers. They help employers select the best candidates for job interviews. They assist both parties in making important employment decisions.

But employers increasingly report how important cover letters are in the hiring process. It's often the accompanying cover letter, rather than the résumé, that clearly separates one candidate from another. Indeed, many individuals get invited to job interviews because of the unique quality of their cover letter. Skilled at writing dynamite cover letters, many of these job seekers also produce other types of great letters—from approach to thank-you—that facilitate their job search.

Become Powerful

Résumés are only as good as the letter accompanying them. Preoccupied with writing good résumés, most job seekers fail to properly introduce their résumé to potential employers. Be forewarned: neglect your cover letter and you may quickly kill your résumé. And failure to write other important job search letters can weaken your job search.

This book is all about acquiring power—increasing your ability to get others to respond to you in positive ways. You have within you the power to shape your future. You can instantly communicate to strangers that you are a professional, competent, thoughtful, and likable individual. You can get others to stand up and take notice of your qualifications. You can get more employers to invite you to job interviews. And you can open more doors to career success.

But you first must take the time and make the effort to clearly communicate, in writing, your qualifications to employers. You must let employers know you are a serious and desirable candidate. You should begin by focusing attention on the needs of your audience and by paying particular attention to the details of powerful communications. That power often begins on paper in the form of dynamite cover letters.

You Are What You Write

❑ **Résumés are only as good as the letter accompanying them. So make sure you write and distribute them right.**

❑ **How and what you write tells potential employers a great deal about your professionalism, competence, and personality. Make sure you pay particular attention to such details when producing your dynamite job search letters.**

❑ **Neglect the importance of a dynamite cover letter–and other types of job search letters–and you neglect one of the most important elements in a successful job search.**

How and what you write tells potential employers a great deal about your professionalism, competence, and personality. Being busy people, employers make quick judgments about you based upon limited information presented to them. Within only a few seconds, your written message motivates them to either select you in or take you out of consideration for a job interview. Neglect the importance of a dynamite cover letter—and other types of job search letters—and you neglect one of the most important elements in a successful job search.

The art of good letter writing is more important than ever in today's busy world where many different channels and mediums of communication must compete for limited attention. When you initially meet strangers through the written word, you essentially are what you write. Readers of your letters draw certain conclusions about your professionalism, competence, and personality based on both the form and content of your written message. If, for example, you write poorly organized and constructed letters, employers will conclude you are probably a disorganized individual. If you make grammatical, spelling, or punctuation errors, employers may conclude you are a careless person who is likely to make errors on the job; or perhaps you lack basic literacy skills. If you type your letter on cheap paper, use a typewriter or dot matrix printer that produces unattractive print, or mass produce your letter on a copy machine, you communicate a lack of class. Worst of all, such choices make the wrong impression on the employer—he or she does not appear important enough to you to warrant a quality presentation of your qualifications. If you fail to accurately address an employer by his or her proper name, title, and address, you communicate other negative messages— you're probably lazy because you didn't take the time to determine to whom the letter should be targeted.

In the end, employers don't want to be bothered with incompetent, inconsiderate, and lazy individuals. They don't want to talk with them nor see them. They definitely have no interest in putting them on their payroll! What they really seek are individuals who are likely to **add value** to their operations and thereby raise the company's I.Q. They examine your written communication for signals of probable value-added behavior. The key question for you is this: *Does my letter and résumé indicate that I will add value to this company?*

Your Writing Skills Do Count

Finding employment in today's job market poses numerous challenges for individuals who seek quality jobs that lead to good salaries, career advancement, and job security. The whole job finding process requires developing and using skills aimed at identifying, contacting, and communicating your qualifications to potential employers. If you want to make this process best work for you, make sure you do more than just mail résumés and letters in response to job vacancies. You must engage in several other job search activities.

To be most successful in finding employment, you need to develop a plan of action that incorporates these seven distinct yet interrelated job search steps or activities:

1. Assess your skills

2. Develop a job/career objective

3. Conduct research on employers and organizations

4. Write résumés and letters

5. Network for information, advice, and referrals

6. Interview for jobs

7. Negotiate salary and terms of employment

As illustrated on page 5, each of these steps involves important **communication skills** involving you and others. Assessing your skills, for example, requires conducting a systematic assessment of what you do well and enjoy doing—your strengths or motivated abilities and skills (MAS) that become translated into your "qualifications" for employers. Conducting research on employers and organizations requires the use of investigative skills commonly associated with library research. Networking and interviewing primarily involve the use of conversational skills—small talk and structured question/answer dialogues—by telephone and in face-to-face encounters.

But it is the critical résumé and letter writing steps that become the major communication challenge for most job seekers. Indeed, your ability to write dynamite cover letters and résumés largely determines how quickly you will transform your job search from the investigative stage (research) to employer contact stages (networking, interviewing, salary negotiations). Your writing skills become the key element in moving your job search from the investigative stage to the final job offer stage.

Let's See Your Paper

> ❑ **Most employers want to see you on paper before meeting you in person.**
>
> ❑ **In a job search aimed at business and professional circles, proper procedures and communication etiquette do count.**

Most employers want to first see you on paper before meeting you in person. In the job search, paper is the great equalizer—you along with many others must pass the written test **before** you can be considered for the face-to-face oral test. Whether you like it or not, you must put your professionalism, competence, and personality in writing before you can be taken seriously for a job. Thus, your writing activities may well become the most critical **transformation step** in your job search. Your writing skills are your ticket to job interviews that lead to job offers.

Job Search Steps and Stages

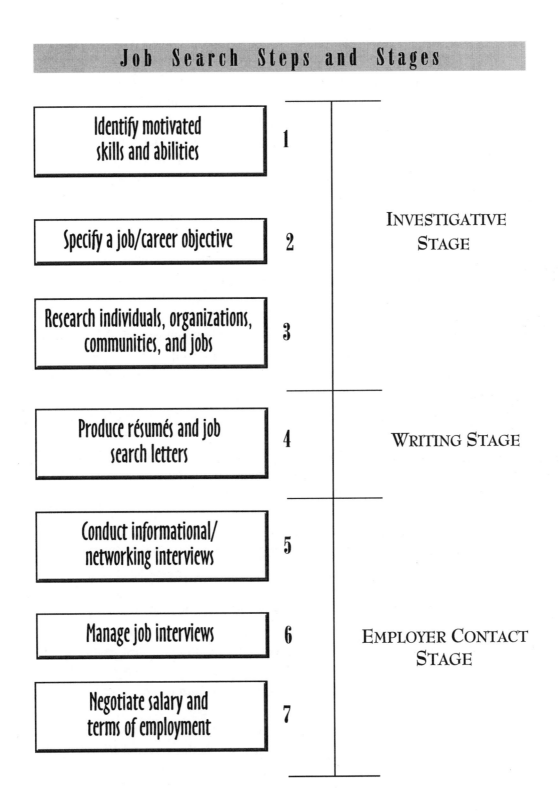

Box	Step		Stage
Identify motivated skills and abilities	1		INVESTIGATIVE STAGE
Specify a job/career objective	2		
Research individuals, organizations, communities, and jobs	3		
Produce résumés and job search letters	4		WRITING STAGE
Conduct informational/ networking interviews	5		EMPLOYER CONTACT STAGE
Manage job interviews	6		
Negotiate salary and terms of employment	7		

For some reason, job search writing skills usually receive little attention beyond the perfunctory *"you must write a résumé and cover letter"* advisory. They also get dismissed as unimportant in a society that supposedly places its greatest value on telecommunicating and interpersonal skills.

Indeed, during the past two decades many career advisors have emphasized networking as the key to getting a job; writing résumés and letters were relatively unimportant job search skills. Some even advised job seekers to dispense with cover letters and résumés altogether and, instead, rely on cold calling telephone techniques and "showing up" networking techniques. Others still accepted the importance of résumés but downplayed the role of cover letters by advising job seekers to put handwritten notes at the top of their résumé in lieu of sending cover letters to potential employers: *"Here's my résumé in response to your vacancy announcement."*

But let's get serious about what's being communicated here. In a job search aimed at business and professional circles, proper procedures and communication etiquette do count. While expedient, such handwritten notes on résumés communicate the wrong messages—you don't take the job nor the employer seriously. Handwritten notes are most appropriately written to subordinates by superiors or to relatives, friends, and acquaintances. And few people have attractive handwriting to complement what should be an attractively printed résumé.

When conducting a serious job search, it is simply inappropriate to treat potential employers as subordinates, relatives, friends, or acquaintances by scribbling a handwritten note on your résumé. They deserve and expect better from strangers who are attempting to persuade them to do something they ordinarily would not do—invite you to a job interview. Being in a position with the power to hire, they expect to receive properly constructed written communications appropriate for their position and indicative of your level of professionalism.

Like much of today's career advice, the scribbled personal note advisory neglects the important role **both** written and interpersonal communication play in the overall job search. Being preoccupied with the "latest technique" for achieving job search success, such advisors fail to see the forest for the trees. They have yet to appreciate the critical **transformation role** written communications play in the larger seven-step job search process.

While some individuals do get interviews by scribbling notes at the top of their résumé, you can do much better if you take the time and effort to craft a thoughtful cover letter. That letter should focus on the employer's needs. It should reinforce the professionalism, competence, and personality which you are ostensibly demonstrating in your attached résumé. Without an effective cover letter, your résumé, as well as the remaining steps in your job search, may have limited impact on potential employers.

Improve Your Effectiveness

Just how effective are you in opening the doors of potential employers? Let's begin by identifying your level of job search information, skills, and strategies as well as those you need to develop and improve. You can do this by completing the following "job search competencies" exercise:

INSTRUCTIONS: Respond to each statement by circling the number on the right that best represents your situation.

SCALE:	1 = strongly agree	4 = disagree
	2 = agree	5 = strongly disagree
	3 = maybe, not certain	

---

1. I know what motivates me to excel at work.   1 2 3 4 5

2. I can identify my strongest abilities and skills.   1 2 3 4 5

3. I can identify at least seven major achievements that
   clarify a pattern of interests and abilities that are
   relevant to my job and career.   1 2 3 4 5

4. I know what I both like and dislike in work.   1 2 3 4 5

5. I know what I want to do during the next 10 years.   1 2 3 4 5

6. I have a well-defined career objective that focuses my
   job search on particular organizations and employers.   1 2 3 4 5

7. I know what skills I can offer employers in
   different occupations.   1 2 3 4 5

8. I know what skills employers most seek in candidates.   1 2 3 4 5

9. I can clearly explain to employers what I do well
   and enjoy doing.   1 2 3 4 5

—continued—

10. I can specify why employers should hire me.   1   2   3   4   5

11. I can gain support of family and friends for making a job or career change.   1   2   3   4   5

12. I can find 10 to 20 hours a week to conduct a part-time job search.   1   2   3   4   5

13. I'm financially capable of sustaining a 3-month job search.   1   2   3   4   5

14. I can conduct library and interview research on different occupations, employers, organizations, and communities.   1   2   3   4   5

15. I can write different types of effective résumés and job search/thank-you letters.   1   2   3   4   5

16. I can produce and distribute résumés and letters to the right people.   1   2   3   4   5

17. I can list my major accomplishments in action terms.   1   2   3   4   5

18. I can identify and target employers with whom I want to interview.   1   2   3   4   5

19. I can develop a job referral network.   1   2   3   4   5

20. I can persuade others to join in forming a job search support group.   1   2   3   4   5

21. I can prospect for job leads.   1   2   3   4   5

22. I can use the telephone to develop prospects and get referrals and interviews.   1   2   3   4   5

23. I can plan and implement an effective direct-mail job search campaign.   1   2   3   4   5

24. I can generate one job interview for every 10 job search contacts I make.   1   2   3   4   5

25. I can follow-up on job interviews.   1   2   3   4   5

26. I can negotiate a salary 10-20% above an initial offer.   1   2   3   4   5

27. I can persuade an employer to renegotiate my salary after six months on the job.   1   2   3   4   5

28. I can create a position for myself in an organization.   1   2   3   4   5

TOTAL   _____

You can calculate your overall job search effectiveness by adding the numbers you circled for a composite score. If your total is more than 75 points, you need to work on developing your job search skills. How you scored each item will indicate to what degree you need to work on improving specific job search skills. If your score is under 50 points, you are well on your way toward job search success. In either case, this book should help you better focus your job search around the critical writing skills necessary for communicating your qualifications to employers. Other books can assist you with many other important aspects of your job search.

Get Taken Seriously By Employers

The whole purpose of a job search is to get taken seriously by strangers who have the power to hire you. Your goal is to both discover and land a job you really want. You do this by locating potential employers and then persuading them to talk to you by telephone and in person about your interests and qualifications.

Being a stranger to most employers, you initially communicate your interests and qualifications on paper in the form of cover letters and résumés. How well you construct these documents will largely determine whether or not you will proceed to the next stage—the job interview.

> **The whole purpose of a job search is to get taken seriously by strangers who have the power to hire you.**

The major weakness of job seekers is their inability to keep focused on their purpose. Engaging in a great deal of wishful thinking, they fail to organize their job search in a purposeful manner. They do silly things, ask dumb questions, and generally waste a great deal of time and money on needless activities. They frustrate themselves by going down the same deadend roads. Worst of all, they turn off employers with their poor communication skills.

The average job seeker often wanders aimlessly in the job market, as if finding a job were an ancient form of alchemy. Preoccupied with job search **techniques**, they lack an overall **purpose and strategy** that would give meaning and direction to discrete job search activities. They often engage in random and time consuming activities that have little or no payoff. Participating in a highly ego-involved activity, they quickly lose sight of what's really important to conducting a successful job search—responding to the needs of employers. Not surprisingly, they aren't taken seriously by employers, because they don't take themselves and the job search serious enough to organize their activities around key communication behaviors that persuade employers to invite them to job interviews. This should not happen to you.

The following pages are designed to increase your power to get taken seriously by employers. Eleven individual chapters show you how to create and distribute dynamite job search letters that command the attention of employers. These chapters:

- Explore numerous myths about cover letters.

- Outline effective writing principles.

- Discuss different types of cover letters.

- Examine the structure of letters.

- Outline effective production and distribution strategies.

- Show how to best implement and follow-up job search letters.

- Present several examples of cover letters and related job search letters.

- Examine the role of faxes, e-mail, and the Internet.

Taken together, these chapters chart important directions your written job search communications should take in reference to employers.

The Product and The Process

While it is tempting to fill the following pages with numerous examples of model letters, such an approach would probably prove ineffective for you. An approach that focuses solely on examples of the **product** implies you should "creatively plagiarize" the examples in order to create effective letters. More importantly, it neglects the whole **process** that is key to job search success— knowing how to organize, produce, distribute, and follow-up each product.

The following chapters focus on the four stages of the letter writing process. Like the job search in general, effective letter writing involves four distinct sequential stages, as illustrated on page 12:

1. Organizing

2. Producing

3. Distributing

4. Following-up

Each stage involves certain principles that contribute to the overall effectiveness of your letters. To be most effective, your letters must adhere to the principles that define each stage. The letter writing stages, in turn, are related to other important job search steps, such as networking and interviewing, which have their own principles for effectiveness. If you follow these steps closely, you should be successful in your job search.

Therefore, the examples in this book are presented to illustrate important **principles** involved in these letter writing stages. They should not be used as examples to be copied or edited. As you will quickly discover, it is extremely important that you craft your own letters that express the "unique you" rather than communicate "canned" messages to potential employers.

In the end, our goal is to improve your communication effectiveness in the job search. On completing this book, you should be able to write dynamite cover letters—as well as other types of job search letters—that result in many more invitations to job interviews.

Do What's Expected and Produces Results

Based on experience, we assume most employers do indeed expect to receive a well-crafted cover letter accompanying an equally well-crafted résumé. We proceed on the assumption that cover letters are just as important as résumés in the job search. In fact, in many cases the cover letter is actually more important than the accompanying résumé. Indeed, employers increasingly report that dynamite cover letters really catch their attention; they persuade them to interview individuals they ordinarily would not have interviewed had they just read their résumé. Such letters stand out from the crowd as they communicate important professional and personal qualities that are difficult to communicate through a resume. Above all, these letters communicate interest, enthusiasm, and intrigue. In essence, they say to the reader: *"You should really get to know me better because I have special qualities that will add value to your operations; I have what you need."*

Effective Letter Writing Process

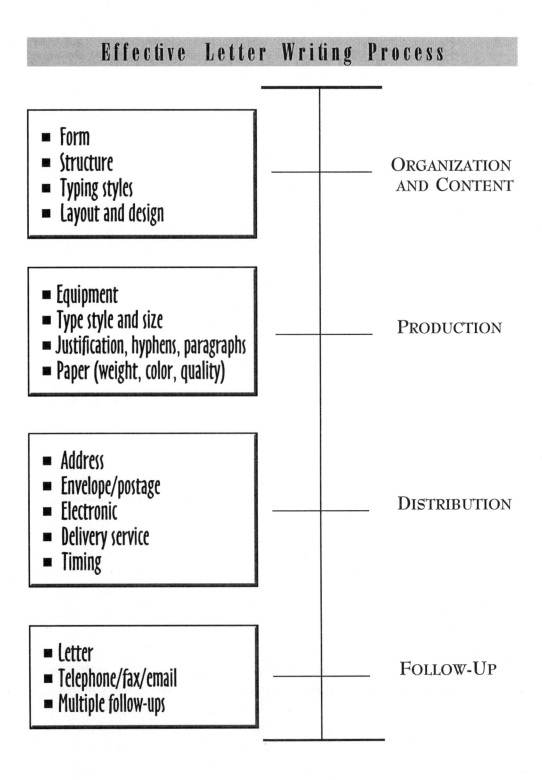

- Form
- Structure
- Typing styles
- Layout and design

ORGANIZATION AND CONTENT

- Equipment
- Type style and size
- Justification, hyphens, paragraphs
- Paper (weight, color, quality)

PRODUCTION

- Address
- Envelope/postage
- Electronic
- Delivery service
- Timing

DISTRIBUTION

- Letter
- Telephone/fax/email
- Multiple follow-ups

FOLLOW-UP

The old interview adage that *"you never have a second chance to make a good first impression"* is equally valid for the cover letter. For it is usually the cover letter rather than your telephone voice or appearance that first introduces you to a prospective employer. Your cover letter tells them who you are and impresses them to spend their valuable time meeting you in person. It enables you to express your personality and style—two important ingredients that are difficult to demonstrate in standard résumé formats. It invites the reader to focus attention on your key qualifications in relation to the employer's needs. It enables you to set an agenda for further exploring your interests and qualifications with employers.

Once you see the importance and function of well-crafted cover letters, you will never again let your résumé reach potential employers without first prefacing it with a dynamite cover letter. For in the end, it may well be your cover letter, rather than your accompanying résumé, that is responsible for getting you invited to the job interview!

Choose the Right Resources

Like its companion *Dynamite Résumés*, this book is primarily concerned with how you can best communicate your qualifications in writing to employers who, in turn, will be sufficiently motivated to invite you to a face-to-face job interview. Several of our other books deal with the additional key steps in the job search process illustrated on page 4: *Change Your Job Change Your Life, Discover the Best Jobs For You, High Impact Résumés and Letters, Dynamite Résumés, Interview For Success, 101 Dynamite Answers to Interview Questions, Dynamite Networking For Dynamite Jobs, Dynamite Tele-Search*, and *Dynamite Salary Negotiations*. Others examine specific career fields, including government hiring processes, public employment strategies, the federal application form, and the special case of educators: *The Complete Guide to Public Employment, Find a Federal Job Fast, The Directory of Federal Jobs and Employers*, and *The Educator's Guide to Alternative Jobs and Careers*. If your interests include the international employment arena, we have three books that can assist you: *The Complete Guide to International Jobs and Careers, The International Jobs Directory*, and *Jobs For People Who Love Travel*. For job alternatives, see our *Best Jobs For the 21st Century* and *Jobs and Careers With Nonprofit Organizations*. These and many other job search books are available directly from Impact Publications. For your convenience, you can order some of these titles by completing the form at the end of this book or by contacting the publisher for a listing of titles.

Impact Publications also publishes a brochure of additional job and career resources. To receive a free copy of this listing, send a self-addressed stamped envelope (#10 business size) to:

IMPACT PUBLICATIONS
ATTN: Career Resource List
9104-N Manassas Drive
Manassas Park, VA 20111-5211

You also may want to visit their Internet site for a complete listing of career resources: *www.impactpublications.com*. Their site contains some of the most important career and job finding resources available today, including many titles that are difficult, if not impossible, to find in bookstores and libraries. You

> **Try this Internet site for the latest information on resources for conducting a dynamite job search:**
> *www.impactpublications.com*

will find everything from additional cover letter books to books on self-assessment, résumés, networking, interviewing, government and international jobs, military, women, minorities, entrepreneurs as well as CD-ROM programs, software, and videos. This is an excellent resource for keeping in touch with the major resources that can assist you with every stage of your job search and with your future career development plans.

Discover Your Paper Power

The art of writing, and writing well, is not widespread in the population. In fact, few people are really good writers who can command the attention and sustain the interest of readers. Many people are more used to picking up the telephone to talk or writing unintelligible notes and cryptic e-mail messages than composing thoughtful letters designed to convey important information and persuade someone to take desired action. When it comes to job search communications, few job seekers know how to communicate their best self in writing to potential employers.

Effective job seekers write dynamite covers letters to accompany their dynamite résumés. Furthermore, they write several other types of job search letters that communicate important professional and personal qualities to potential employers.

The pages that follow are designed to put more power into your job search by developing dynamite cover letters and other types of written job search communications. Join us as we take you through the letter writing maze that can substantially improve your chances of being called for an interview that leads to a job offer. Like many other job seekers, you may soon discover your own letter power: it's the quality of your letters, along with your résumé, that leads to job interviews. Thus, writing powerful letters should become one of your top priority job search activities.

2

Myths and Realities

Conducting an effective job search requires a clear understanding of the job market and how to use effective job search strategies and techniques. Unfortunately, many individuals approach the job market with numerous myths about how it operates as well as misconceptions concerning the most effective methods for achieving success. Many of these myths relate to the role of cover letters and résumés in the job search.

Let's examine several myths that are likely to prevent you from taking effective action in today's job market. These myths, along with corresponding realities, outline a set of important **principles** for best communicating your qualifications to potential employers. They illustrate important points for organizing each step of your job search.

The Job Search

Myths	Realities
1. Anyone can find a job; all you need to know is how to find a job.	This "form versus substance" myth is often associated with career counselors who were raised on popular career planning exhortations of the 1970s and 1980s that stressed the importance of having

16

positive attitudes and self-esteem, setting goals, dressing for success, and using interpersonal strategies for finding jobs. While such approaches may work well in an industrial society with low unemployment, they constitute myths in a post-industrial, high-tech society which requires employees to demonstrate both **intelligence and concrete work skills** as well as a **willingness to relocate** to new communities offering greater job opportunities. For example, many of today's unemployed are highly skilled in the old technology of the industrial society, but they live and own homes in economically depressed communities. These people lack the necessary **skills and mobility** required for getting jobs in high-tech, growth communities. Knowing job search skills alone will not help these people. Indeed, such advice and knowledge will most likely frustrate such highly motivated individuals who possess skills appropriate for old technology.

2. **The best way to find a job is to respond to classified ads, use employment agencies, and submit applications to personnel offices.**

   Except for certain types of organizations, such as government, these formal application procedures are not the most effective ways of finding jobs. Such approaches assume the presence of an organized, coherent, and centralized job market—but no such thing exists. The job market is highly decentralized, fragmented, and chaotic. Classified ads, employment agencies, and personnel offices tend to list low paying yet highly competitive jobs. Most of the best jobs—high level, excellent pay, least competitive—are neither listed nor advertised; they are found through word-of-mouth. Your most fruitful strategy will be to conduct research and informational interviews on what career counselors call the "hidden job market."

3. **Few jobs are available for me in today's competitive job market.**

   This may be true if you lack marketable skills and insist on applying for jobs listed with newspapers, employment agencies, or personnel offices. Competition in the advertised job market is high, especially for jobs requiring few skills. Jobs with little competition are available on the hidden job market.

Jobs requiring advanced technical skills often go begging. Little competition may occur during periods of high unemployment, because many people quit job hunting after a few disappointing weeks of working the advertised job market.

4. **I know how to find a job, but opportunities are not available for me.**

Most people don't know how to find a job, some lack marketable job skills, and they fail to clearly communicate their qualifications to employers. They continue to use ineffective job search methods. Opportunities are readily available for those who understand the structure and operation of the job market, have appropriate work-content skills, use job search methods designed for the hidden job market, and are skilled in communicating their qualifications to employers.

5. **Employers are in the driver's seat; they have the upper-hand with applicants.**

Most often no one is in the driver's seat. Not knowing what they want, many employers make poor hiring decisions. They frequently let applicants define their hiring needs as the applicant's strengths and capabilities. If you, too, can define employers' needs as your skills, you might end up in the driver's seat!

6. **Employers hire the best qualified candidates. Without a great deal of experience and numerous qualifications, I don't have a chance.**

Employers hire people for all kinds of reasons. Most rank experience and qualifications third or fourth in their pecking order of hiring criteria. Employers seldom hire the best qualified candidate, because "qualifications" are difficult to define and measure. Employers normally seek people with the following characteristics: competent, intelligent, honest, and likeable. "Likability" tends to be an overall concern of employers. Employers want **value** for their money. Therefore, you must communicate to employers in writing, over the telephone, and in person that you are such an individual. You must overcome employers' objections to any lack of experience or qualifications. But never volunteer your weaknesses. The best qualified person is the one who knows how to get the job—convinces employers that he or she is the **most** desirable for the job.

7. **It is best to go into a growing field where jobs are plentiful.**

Be careful in following the masses into today's so-called hot "in" fields. People who primarily pursue occupations for money, status, position, or perceived future job growth (objective opportunities) rather than for compatibility with their interests and skills (the right "fit") may be in for many career disappointments. First, many of today's glamorous go-go growth fields can quickly experience no-growth as well as major cutbacks—such as aerospace engineering, nuclear energy, architecture, real estate, and defense contracting—when the economy shifts into a recessionary mode or industries experience serious challenges. Second, by the time you acquire the necessary skills for entry into these occupations, you may experience the recurring "disappearing job" phenomenon: too many people did the same thing you did and consequently glut the job market about the time you are ready to enter the job market. Many students completing law degrees, for example, have been recent casualties of such a job market. Third, since many people leave no-growth fields, new opportunities may arise for you in these fields. Fourth, if you go after a growth field, you will try to fit into a job rather than find a job fit for you. If you know what you do well and enjoy doing and what additional training you may need, you should look for a job conducive to your particular mix of skills, interests, and motivations. In the long-run you will be happier and more productive finding a job fit for you.

8. **People over 40 have difficulty finding a good job.**

Yes, if they apply for youth and entry-level jobs. Age should be an insignificant barrier to employment if you conduct a well organized job search and are prepared to handle this potential negative with employers. Age should be a positive and must be communicated as such. After all, employers want experience, maturity, and stability. People over 40 generally possess these qualities. As the population ages and birth rates decline, older individuals should have a much easier time changing jobs and careers.

9. **I must be aggressive in order to find a job.**

Many aggressive people also tend to be offensive and obnoxious people. Try being purposeful, persistent, and pleasant in all your job search activities. Such behavior is well received by potential employers.

10. **I should not change jobs and careers more than once or twice. Job-changers are discriminated against in hiring.**

While this may have been generally true 30 years ago, it is no longer true today. America is a skills-based society: individuals market their skills to organizations in exchange for money and position. Furthermore, since most organizations are small businesses with limited advancement opportunities, careers quickly plateau for most people. For them, the only way up is to get out and into another organization. Therefore, the best way to advance careers in a society of small businesses is to change jobs. Job-changing is okay as long as such changes demonstrate career advancement and one isn't changing jobs every few months. Most individuals entering the job market today will undergo several career and job changes regardless of their initial desire for a one-job, one-career life plan.

11. **People get ahead by working hard and putting in long hours.**

Success patterns differ. Many people who are honest, work hard, and put in long hours also get fired, have ulcers, and die young. Some people get ahead even though they are dishonest and lazy. Others simply have good luck or a helpful patron. Moderation in both work and play will probably get you just as far as the extremes. There are other ways to become successful in addition to hard work and long hours.

12. **I should not try to use contacts or connections to get a job. I should apply through the front door like everyone else. If I'm the best qualified, I'll get the job.**

While you may wish to stand in line for tickets, bank deposits, and loans—because you have no clout with the front office—standing in line for a job is dumb. Every employer has a front door as well as a back door. Try using the back door if you can. It works in many cases.

Cover Letters

Several additional myths and realities directly relate to cover letters in the job search. Most are communication myths that fail to appreciate the importance of **consistently projecting a professional image** at all stages of a job search. Among the most important myths are the following:

Myths	Realities

13. **Résumés and networking are more important to getting a job than cover letters.**

We really don't know what actions produce the most important results for getting a job in any specific individual case. While résumés and networking are important, so too are well-crafted cover letters and telephone and face-to-face interviews. Many employers report that impressive cover letters are often more important than résumés in making decisions to interview candidates.

14. **The purpose of a cover letter is to introduce your résumé to an employer.**

A cover letter should be much more than mere cover for a résumé. Indeed, it may be a misnomer to call these letters "cover letters." It's best to think of these letters as "interview generating" communications. The purpose of a cover letter should be to get the employer to **take action** on your résumé. Consequently, the whole structure of your cover letter should focus on persuading the employer to invite you for a job interview.

15. A cover letter should be only one paragraph in length.

Cover letters should say something about you to the employer. While you should try to keep your letter short and to the point, don't limit it to a few lines. Remember what you are trying to do—get the employer to take action in reference to your interests and qualifications as partially outlined in your résumé. A well constructed cover letter should be organized like advertising copy:

- catch the reader's attention
- persuade the reader about you (you are the product)
- convince the reader with more evidence
- move the reader to acquire your service or you

Since you need to accomplish a great deal in your letter, this letter will probably run three paragraphs and be confined to one page.

16. It's okay to send your résumé to an employer without an accompanying cover letter.

Only if you want the employer to think his or her position and employment opportunity are not important. This myth is propagated by those who believe employers are too busy to read but not too busy to be pestered by telephone calls and networkers who invite themselves to interviews. Employers initially prefer succinct written communications. It enables them to screen candidates in and out for the next stage of the hiring process —a telephone screening interview. Sending a résumé without a cover letter is like going to a job interview barefoot—your application is incomplete and your résumé is not being properly communicated for taking action. Cover letters should always accompany résumés that are sent through the mail. They help position your interests and qualifications in relation to the employer's needs as well as indicate what action will be taken next. Above all, they give employers signals of your personality, style, and likability—important elements in the hiring decision.

17. **If you don't have a name, it's okay to address your cover letter to the Director of Personnel or "To Whom It May Concern."**

Your cover letter should be addressed to the person responsible for making the hiring decision, which most likely is not the Director of Personnel. Individuals in personnel are normally responsible for announcing vacancies, processing applications, and managing day-to-day personnel matters. What hiring they do is primarily confined to positions within their own unit or deal with lower level support positions that service many operating units. Hiring decisions for most positions are usually made in the operating units rather than in personnel. Always address your letter to a specific person—by name and position—and address them as Mr., Mrs., or Ms. If you don't have a name, call the organization and ask to whom you should address your communications.

18. **Sending a general cover letter and résumé to hundreds of employers will increase my chances of getting a job.**

Such a non-focused shotgun approach will initially give you a false sense of making progress with your job search because it involves a major expenditure of time and money. But it will most likely increase your level of frustration when you receive few replies and numerous rejections. This approach is nothing more than playing a game of probability where your probabilities are extremely low—a 2 percent response rate would be considered excellent! It's always best to target your résumé on specific jobs, organizations, and individuals. A general "To Whom It May Concern" cover letter is destined for the circular files. It indicates you did not take the time to learn about the organization nor the employer's needs. Such random behavior indicates you are not a thoughtful and serious person. Worse still, you appear desperate for a job. How many employers are eager to hire such people?

19. **Handwritten letters have a greater impact on employers than typewritten letters.**

Handwritten cover letters are inappropriate as are scribbled notes on or attached to a résumé. They are **too** personal and look unprofessional when applying for a job. If you are a professional, you want to demonstrate that you can present yourself to others in the most professional manner possible. Confine your handwriting activities to your signature only. The letter should be typed on a good quality machine—preferably a letter quality printer. An exception to this rule is in the case of applying for a job in Europe. European employers prefer handwritten cover letters. Indeed, they even go so far as to analyze your handwriting as part of the screening process!

20. **Your cover letter should summarize your résumé, highlight your major strengths, and invite the employer to call you on the telephone for an interview.**

Such a cover letter would be unnecessarily redundant, long, and probably boring. Remember, the goal of your cover letter is to answer the key question facing the employer you wish to interview with: "Why should I invite this person to an interview and perhaps hire her or him?" Your answers should be immediately evident—preferably in the first paragraph—short, and to the point.

21. **Include your salary history and expectations in your cover letter as well as your references.**

Never volunteer salary information in writing nor so early in the application process; answers to this question should come near the end of the job interview, when you negotiate salary **after** receiving a job offer. Only include it if the employer specifically requests that your salary history and expectations be included in writing. And when you do, avoid stating a specific salary figure. State "negotiable" or give a **salary range** which should accurately reflect the value of both the position and you. Salary is something that should be **negotiated** at the very end of your job interview. The same principle applies to references. Volunteer your references only upon request, which is often during the interview. Never include them in your cover letter nor on your résumé. If you are specifically asked to supply a list of references, do so, but make sure you have contacted the individuals named as your references and briefed them about your job search and this specific position. They should be prepared for an expected phone call from the prospective employer.

22. **Always end your letter with an indication that you expect to hear from the employer: "I look forward to hearing from you."**

What do you expect will happen when you close your letter in this manner? Probably nothing. While this is a polite and acceptable way of closing such a letter, it is a rather empty statement of hope—not one of action. Remember, you always want **action** to result from your written communication. Any type of action—positive or negative— should help you move on to the next stage of your job search with this or other potential employers. This standard closing is likely to result in no action on the part of the employer who is by definition a busy person. It's better to indicate that **you** will take initiative in contacting the employer in response to your letter and résumé. End your letter with an action statement like this one:

> I'll give you a call Thursday afternoon to answer any questions you may have regarding my interests and qualifications.

Such an action statement, in effect, invites you to a telephone interview—the first step to getting a face-to-face job interview. While some employers may avoid your telephone call, at least you will get some action in reference to your letter and résumé. If, for example, you call on Thursday afternoon and the employer is not available to take your call, leave a message that you called in reference to your letter. Chances are the employer is expecting your call and will remember you because you are taking this initiative. In some cases, the employer will tell you frankly that you are no longer under consideration. While disappointing, this rejection has a positive side—it clarifies your status so you no longer need to waste your time nor engage in wishful thinking about the status of your application with this employer. Go on to others who may prove more responsive. In other cases, your phone call may result in getting a face-to-face interview early on in the application process with this employer. Taking action in this manner will at least give you useful information that will bring your application nearer to closure. But make sure you call at the time you say you will call. If the employer expects your call on Thursday afternoon and you forget to call, you prematurely communicate a negative message to the employer—you lack follow-through. Always do what you say you will do and in a timely fashion.

23. Sign your full name.

What's in a name? A lot. Particular names generate certain positive and negative images amongst employers who are screening strangers for interviews. While most people are content with their inherited name, others might consider changing their name, especially if it is a real negative to their career. Whether you use just your first and last name or include a middle initial depends on your professional style. In general, the use of a full first name and middle initial tends to communicate a more formal and professional style; it tends to create greater distance between you and the employer. A shortened first name (Bill rather than William, or Jenny rather than Jennifer) tends to communicate an informal style and greater social openness. If you have an unusual name that may distract from your qualifications, such as Kitty Kat, Flagler Finch, or Foxy Trot, consider doing something about it—a formal name change may be in order if it appears negative to your career! We too often come across unusual and sometimes hilarious names that prevent individuals from being taken seriously by employers. While your parents may have had fun naming you as a cute baby, life is a more serious business. Whatever you do, try to communicate your particular style in your name, knowing full well employers are looking for serious people.

24: Sign your letter in black ink.

Again, your signature should indicate your professional style. Black ink is okay, but blue looks better in contrast to black type. It's better to use a fountain pen rather than a ballpoint pen for signing your name—if you can write neatly with a fountain pen. Fountain pen ink communicates more class and indicates a certain professional style desired by many employers.

25. **It's best to produce your cover letter and other job search letters on a typewriter.**

Try to keep the type style of your cover letter the same as your résumé. Ideally, produce both your cover letter and résumé on a word processor using the same printer. Avoid dot matrix printers which look unprofessional and indicate computer-generated mass mailings. If you use a desktop publishing program that allows you to choose different type styles for a laser printer, choose Times Roman, Palatino, New Century, ITC Bookman, or a similar standard type style; avoid Helvetica or an italicized script which are difficult to read. Use nothing less than a letter quality printer. If you use a typewriter, make sure it produces top quality type and is error free—do not erase, use white-out, or apply chalk correcting tape to fix typing errors. Avoid machines that produce amateurish looking or messy type; the type should look neat, clean, and sharp. If you lack in-house capabilities to produce such quality documents, contact someone who does. Many people specialize in producing quality documents at reasonable rates. Do not short-change your job search by producing sloppy and amateurish looking cover letters and résumés.

26. **Produce your cover letter on off-white paper.**

While paper colors do make a difference in communicating professional styles, there is nothing magical about ivory or off-white paper. As more and more people use this color, the off-white color has lost its effectiveness. Try a light grey or basic white. Indeed, white paper gives a nice bright look to what has become essentially a dull colored process. If you are applying for a creative position, you may want to use more daring colors to better express your creative style and personality.

27. **Paper quality is not important as long as you type your letter neatly and choose a proper paper color.**

Paper quality expressed in terms of weight and texture does make a difference. It, too, communicates something about your professional style and personality. Stay with a 20 to 50 pound bond paper that has the look and feel of a professional document. You achieve the proper look and feel by using 100% cotton fiber or "rag content" paper. Avoid very thin or thick and coarse papers.

28. **Use personalized stationery with your name, address, and phone number printed across the top.**

While printed personalized stationery looks nice, it's not necessary to go to such an extreme to impress employers. It may be a negative to some employers who think you may be a bit extravagant. It's quite acceptable to produce your letter in a standard blank piece of quality paper; type your return address at the top where it should normally go depending on the letter style you choose.

29. **Sending your letter and résumé by special next-day delivery services—Express Mail, UPS Next Day Air, Federal Express, or courier service—will increase your chances of getting an interview.**

This may be another case of overkill that primarily demonstrates your extravagance in using expensive delivery arrangements rather than result in having a positive impact on the employer's decision-making. While these services will get your cover letter and résumé quickly in the hands of the employer, they may not make much of a difference. After all, employers are not prepared to make their decisions on the day your mailing arrives. It's fine to send your communications by first-class mail.

30. **It's best to have machine imprinted postage applied to the envelope rather than use stamps.**

We're not sure which type of postage works best. To be on a safe side, use a stamp rather than machine imprinted postage. A stamp—preferably an attractive commemorative stamp—looks nice and is more personal than machine imprinted postage. In fact, many people report better responses to letters mailed with stamps. If you use machine imprinted postage, an employer may think you are abusing your present employer's postage machine. Under no circumstances should you send your letters by bulk mail—stamp, machine imprinted, or indicia. Such mailings communicate two negatives—you are engaged in mass mailings and thus not serious about this employer, and you are cheap. The same holds true for affixing mailing labels to envelopes. All information on the front of an envelope should be typed. Mailing labels are impersonal and communicate "junk mail" and laziness. You may have rented a mailing list consisting of numerous employers!

31. **It's best to send your cover letter and résumé in a matching No. 10 business envelope.**

A No. 10 business envelope requires you to fold your cover letter and résumé at least twice. At the receiving end, it requires the employer to unfold it twice and then try to keep it flat in a pile of other similarly folded documents. A non-folded cover letter and résumé stands out better in a pile of partly folded documents. We recommend sending your 8 x 11½ cover letter and résumé in a 9 x 12 white envelope. Try to find a good quality envelope in this size. Stamp, handwrite, or affix a label that says "First Class" or "Priority" one inch above the left hand corner of the address.

32. **Follow-up your cover letter with a copy of the original letter accompanied by a handwritten note in the upper right hand corner inquiring about the status of your application.**

This approach lacks class. Always try to follow-up with a telephone call. You should have indicated in the final paragraph of your letter that you would make this call at a specific time. But don't expect to make direct contact with your first phone call. If your first telephone follow-up call fails to put you in contact with the employer, make another three to seven calls until you make direct contact. Keep your cool if your calls aren't returned—many people simply don't return their calls. If after seven calls you still can't get through, write a follow-up letter inquiring about the status of your application and mention your continuing interest in the position. But do not just send another copy of your letter.

33. **It's best to fax or e-mail letters and résumés these days to busy employers than to send them by s-nail mail.**

Only fax or e-mail a letter and/or résumé if requested to do so by an employer. While faxes and e-mail are efficient ways of communicating, they are not necessarily the most effective. Most people do not appreciate unsolicited faxes and e-mail. Indeed, if you want to quickly take yourself out of consideration, start faxing and e-mailing your job search communication. Also, more and more studies show that employers are more likely to respond to traditional mailed letters than to e-mail. Indeed, many people do not consider e-mail to be serious, professional communication.

While conducting your job search, you will encounter many of these and other myths and realities about how to best communicate your qualifications to employers. Several people will give you advice. While much of this advice will be useful, a great deal of it will be useless and misleading. You should be skeptical of well-meaning individuals who most likely will reiterate the same myths. You should be particularly leery of those who try to **sell** you their advice.

Always remember you are entering a relatively disorganized and chaotic job market where you can find numerous job opportunities. Your task is to organize the chaos around your skills and interests. You must convince prospective employers that they will like you more than other "qualified" candidates. A well-crafted cover letter that is properly produced, distributed, and followed up will play a key role in communicating your qualifications to employers.

3

Essential Job Search Letters

Written communications should play an important role throughout your job search. Not only do you introduce yourself to prospective employers by writing résumés and cover letters, you also should direct other types of letters to potential employers.

The most important job search letters are cover, approach, thank-you, and résumé letters. Each of these letters can be subdivided into additional types of letters. Let's survey these letters before we examine the details of writing and distributing dynamite cover letters.

Cover Letters

The cover letter is a special type of job search letter. By definition, it always accompanies a résumé and usually is targeted toward potential employers.

Employers regularly receive two types of cover letters—targeted and broadcast. Each letter provides cover for an enclosed résumé.

TARGETED COVER LETTER

The targeted cover letter is the most commonly written job search letter. It is addressed to a specific person and in reference to a position which may or may

31

not be vacant. It may be written in response to a classified ad or vacancy announcement or in reference to a job lead received from a referral.

A targeted cover letter should be specific and oriented toward the needs of the employer. The content of this letter should reflect as much knowledge of the employer and the position as possible. The writer should emphasize his or her skills that appear most compatible with the needs of the employer and the requirements of the position. It should tell the employer why he or she should take time to talk with you by telephone or meet you in person to further discuss your qualifications. It should communicate both professional and personal qualities about you—you are a competent **and** likable individual.

> ❑ **The most important job search letters are cover, approach, thank-you, and résumé letters.**
>
> ❑ **The targeted cover letter is the most commonly written job search letter.**
>
> ❑ **Always try to address your targeted letter to a specific person, by name and title. Avoid generic titles that do little to enhance your credibility.**
>
> ❑ **The targeted cover letter is designed to directly connect you to the needs of the employer.**

Always try to **address this letter to a specific person**, by name and title. A proper salutation should begin with Mr., Mrs., or Ms. If you are unclear whether you are writing to a male or female, because of the unisex nature of the first name or the use of initials only—Darrell Smith or L. C. Williams—use "Mr." or the full name—"Dear Darrell Smith" or "Dear L. C. Williams." Women should always be addressed as "Ms." unless you know for certain that "Mrs." or "Miss" is the appropriate and preferred salutation. However, many classified ads and vacancy announcements only include an address. Some may appear to be blind ads with limited information on the employer—P.O. Box 7999, Culver City, CA. If you are unable to determine to whom to address your letter, use one of two preferred choices:

1. "Dear Sir or Madam" or "Dear Sir/Madam." This is the formal, neutral, and most acceptable way of addressing an anonymous reader.

2. Eliminate this perfunctory salutation altogether and go directly from the inside address to the first paragraph, leaving three spaces between the two sections. We prefer this "open" style since it directs your letter to the organization in the same manner in which the anonymous classified ad or vacancy announcement was addressed. Your opening sentence will indicate to whom the letter goes.

Whatever your choices, please do not address the individual as "Dear Gentleperson," "Dear Gentlepeople," "Dear Person," "Dear Sir," "Dear Future Employer," "Dear Friend," "Dear Company," "Dear Personnel Department," or "To Whom It May Concern." Employers are neither gentlepeople nor friends; a "sir" often turns out to be a female; you should not be so presumptuous to imply you'll be working there soon; and a company or department is not a person. Such salutations do nothing to elevate your status in the eyes of a potential employer. Several are negatives; most verge on being dumb! It's perfectly acceptable to follow the time-honored rule of *"When in doubt, leave it out."*

The targeted cover letter is designed to directly **connect** you to the needs of the employer. It is normally divided into three distinct paragraphs. In response to a classified ad or vacancy announcement, for example, the first paragraph of this letter should connect you to the advertised position by way of introduction. For openers, make your first sentence connect you directly to the employer's advertising efforts:

> The sales and marketing position you advertised in today's Record-Courier coincides nicely with my interests and experience.

The remaining sentences should connect your skills and goals to the position and organization:

> The sales and marketing position you advertised in today's Record-Courier coincides nicely with my interests and experience. I have seven years of progressive sales and marketing experience in pharmaceuticals, involving $3.5 million in annual sales. I'm interested in taking on new challenges with a highly respected and innovative pharmaceutical firm that values team performance and wishes to explore new markets.

Such an opening paragraph is short, to the point, grabs attention, and avoids the canned language and droning character of so many boring and pointless cover letters received by hiring personnel. Our letter emphasizes four key points:

- Where and when you learned about the position—you make a logical and legitimate connection to the employer. Also, employers like to know where candidates learn about the vacancy in order to determine the effectiveness of their advertising campaigns.

- You have specific skills and experience directly related to the employer's needs.

- You are interested in this position because you want to progress in your career rather than because of need (you're unemployed) or greed (you want more money). Your purpose is both employer- and career-centered rather than self-centered.

- Your style and tone is professional, personal, positive, upbeat, and value neutral. Most important, you appear "likable." You avoid making canned, self-serving, or flattering statements about yourself and the employer. The reader is probably impressed so far with your skills, interests, and knowledge of his or her firm. The reader's initial response is to learn more about you by reading the rest of the letter as well as reviewing the enclosed résumé.

If you send a cover letter and résumé in response to a referral, the only change in reference to our first original targeted cover letter (page 51) involves the first sentence (page 52). In this case you may or may not be responding to a specific position vacancy. An employer may be surveying existing talent to see what's available to the organization for possible personnel expansion. This is an example of how an employer may hire someone without ever advertising a vacancy—behavior in the so-called "hidden job market." He or she may want to let the market determine whether or not the organization is interested in adding new personnel. In this cover letter, the emphasis again is on making a legitimate connection to the employer. The tone is more personal:

> Jane Parsons, who spoke with you on Friday about my interests, suggested I contact you about my sales and marketing experience. She said you wished to see my résumé.
>
> I have seven years of progressive sales and marketing experience in pharmaceuticals, involving $3.5 million in annual sales. I'm interested in taking on new challenges with a highly respected and innovative pharmaceutical firm that values team performance and wishes to explore new markets.

This is the best type of referral you can receive—an intermediary already introduced you to a potential employer who is requesting your résumé. She has already legitimized your candidacy and screened your qualifications based on her own judgment and personal relationship with the employer. If she is highly respected by the employer for her judgment on personnel matters—or better still if the employer "owes her a favor"—you have an important foot in the door. At this point you need to reinforce her judgment with a well-crafted cover letter and résumé immediately followed up with a phone call. In this case you need not mention a specific position being advertised since it may not actually be advertised. Include only the name of your referral as well as refer to those interests and skills you already know are compatible with the employer's interests. Keep in mind that the opening sentence—personal reference to your referral—is the most important element in this letter.

The remaining paragraphs in this type of targeted letter will follow the same form used for other kinds of cover letters—emphasize your relevant experience and skills, which are summarized in your résumé, and call for action on your candidacy. We'll examine these other paragraphs later.

BROADCAST COVER LETTER

Broadcast cover letters are the ultimate exercise in delivering job search junk mail to employers. These letters are produced by job search dreamers. These are basically form letters sent to hundreds, perhaps thousands, of employers in the hope of being "discovered" by someone in need of your particular qualifications and experience. This is a favorite marketing method used by job search firms that charge individuals to help them find a job. It is their single most important indicator—however ineffective—that they are performing for their clients. The broadcast cover letter and résumé proves to their clients that they are doing something for them in exchange for their fees: *"This week we sent 1,500 copies of your résumé to our in-house list of employers."* Many paying clients actually believe they are getting their money's worth. Perhaps in a few days a job will be in the mail for them!

Many job hunters resort to sending such letters because the broadcast exercise involves motion. It gives them a feeling of doing something about their job search—they are actually contacting potential employers with their résumé —without having to go through the process of making personal contacts through referrals and cold calls. Like most direct-mail schemes engaged in by the uninitiated, this is the lazy person's way to job search riches. Just find the names and addresses of several hundred potential employers, address the envelopes and affix postage, and then stuff them with your résumé and cover letter. Presto! In a few days you expect phone calls from employers who just discovered your talents by opening their junk mail!

Let's speak the truth about going nowhere with this approach. Motion does not mean momentum. Anyone who thinks he or she can get a job by engaging in such a junk mail exercise is at best engaging in a self-fulfilling prophecy: it results in few if any responses and numerous rejections. If you want to experience rejections, or need to fill your weekly depression quota, just broadcast several hundred résumés and letters to employers. Wait a few weeks and you will most likely get the depressing news—no one is positive about you and your résumé. At best you will receive a few polite form letters informing you that the employer will keep your résumé on file:

> Thank you for sending us your résumé. While we do not have a vacancy at present for someone with your qualifications, we will keep your résumé on file for future reference.

If after receiving several such replies you conclude it's a tough job market out there, and no one is interested in your qualifications and experience, you're probably correct. Such an approach to communicating your qualifications to employers simply sets you up for failure. You probably don't need this type of compounding experience!

This is not to say that this approach never works. Indeed, some people do get job interviews from such broadcasted cover letters and résumés. The reason they get interviews is not because of the quality of their résumé, letter, or mailing list. It's because of dumb luck in playing the numbers game.

> **Broadcast cover letters are the ultimate exercise in delivering junk mail to employers. They represent one of the least effective job search approaches.**

Direct-mail operates like this. If you know what you are doing—have an excellent product targeted to a very receptive audience—you may receive a 2% positive response. Indeed, successful direct-mail campaigns use 2% as an indicator of success. On the other hand, if your product is less than exciting and is not well targeted on an audience, you can expect to receive less than .5% positive response. In some cases you may receive no response whatsoever. In fact, few direct-mail campaigns ever result in a 2% response rate!

You should never expect to receive more than a 1% positive response to your broadcast letters and résumés. Translated into real numbers, this means for every 100 unsolicited résumés you mail, you'll be lucky to get one interview. For every 1000 résumés you mail, you may get 10 interviews. But you will be lucky if you even get a 1% positive response. Chances are your efforts will be rewarded with no invitations to interview.

The reason for such meager numbers is simple: you don't have a receptive audience for your mailing piece. Employers are busy and serious people who seek candidates when they have specific personnel needs. If they have no vacancies, why would they be interested in interviewing candidates or even replying to an unsolicited letter and résumé for a nonexistent position? Such mail is a waste of their time. Writing responses to such mail costs them time and money. Employers simply don't interview people based upon a survey of their junk mail. And they don't feel obligated to respond to unsolicited mail.

If you do get an interview from a broadcast letter, chances are you got lucky: your letter and résumé arrived at the time an employer was actually looking for a candidate with your type of qualifications. This is best termed "dumb luck."

If you decide to engage in the broadcast exercise, please don't waste a great deal of time and money trying to produce the "perfect" mailing piece or acquiring a "hot" mailing list. It's wishful thinking that the quality of the mailing piece or your mailing list will somehow give you an "extra edge" in generating a higher response rate.

Simply write a short three-paragraph cover letter in which you generate interest in both you and your résumé as well as demonstrate your enthusiasm, drive, honesty, goals, and performance orientation. The first two paragraphs introduce you to the employer by way of your experience, previous performance, and future goals. The final paragraph calls for action on the part of the receiver:

> I have seven years of progressive sales and marketing experience in pharmaceuticals. Last year alone I generated $3.5 million in annual sales—a 25% increase over the previous year. Next year I want to do at least $4.5 million.
>
> I'm interested in taking on new challenges with a firm that values team performance and is interested in exploring new markets. As you can see from my enclosed résumé, I have extensive sales and marketing experience. For the past five years, I've exceeded my annual sales goals.
>
> If you have a need for someone with my experience, I would appreciate an opportunity to speak with you about my qualifications and future plans. I can be contacted during the day at 808/729-3290 and in the evening at 808/729-4751.

If this letter were received by an employer who had a specific need for an experienced and productive individual in pharmaceutical sales and marketing, chances are he or she would contact the writer. However, the chances are very slim that this letter would connect with an employer who had such an immediate and specific need. Therefore, this otherwise excellent letter is likely to result in numerous rejections because it has no audience on the day it arrives.

While it is always preferable to address your letter to a specific name and type each envelope rather than use computer-generated mailing labels, in the end it probably doesn't really make much difference if no position exists in reference to your letter and résumé. It does make a difference if you are lucky to stumble upon a position through such a mailing effort. An employer either does or does not have a personnel need specifically coinciding with your qualifications and experience. The **content** of both your letter and résumé is the most important element in this broadcast exercise. If an employer has a specific personnel need and your letter and résumé indicate you fit those needs, you'll probably hear from the employer, regardless of whether you have his or her correct name and title or if you used a computer-generated mailing label. The employer knows what you are doing regardless of any cosmetic pretenses to the contrary.

> ❏ **Approach letters are used for gaining information, advice, and referrals.**
>
> ❏ **Never include your résumé with an approach letter. It sends the wrong message and thus diminishes the effectiveness of your letter.**
>
> ❏ **The most effective approach letter is one based on a referral. This type of letter plays a central role in the networking process.**
>
> ❏ **Include an action statement at the end of your letter—state when you will call the recipient.**
>
> ❏ **Be sure to always follow-up your approach letters with telephone calls.**

How effective this mailing piece becomes will depend on your luck. Whatever you do, don't expect to receive many positive responses. And be prepared for an avalanche of bad news—no one appears to want you! You will collect numerous rejections in the process. After you complete this direct mail exercise, get back to what you should really be doing with your job search time—directly contacting potential employers through referral networks, cold calling techniques, and in response to advertised vacancies. Cover letters targeted to employers with specific personnel needs will result in many more positive responses than the junk mail you generated. You will decrease your number of rejections with a higher number of acceptances.

Approach Letters

Approach letters are some of the most important letters you should write during your job search. The purpose of these letters is to approach individuals for job search information, advice, and referrals. They play a central role in your prospecting and networking activities. You write them because you need information on alternative jobs, the job market, organizations, potential employers, and job vacancies. You need this information because the job market is highly decentralized and chaotic, and because you want to uncover job leads before others learn about them. Approach letters help you bring some degree of coherence and structure to your job search by organizing the job market around your interests, skills, and experience.

Approach letters are largely responsible for opening doors for **informational interviews**—one of the most critical interviews in your job search. Approach letters help give you access to important job information and potential employers. Failure to write these letters is likely to weaken your overall job search campaign.

One of the most important differences between approach letters and cover letters is that an approach letter should **never** be accompanied by a résumé. The reason is simple: an enclosed résumé implies you are looking for a job from the individual who receives your letter. You put responsibility on this individual to either give you a job or help you find one. Few individuals want such responsibility or are eager to become your job search helper. This pushy and presumptuous approach violates the most important principle of the approach letter—these letters are designed for gaining access to critical job search information, advice, and referrals. Such a letter should never imply that you are looking for a job with or through this individual. It's only during an informational interview—preferably **after** you receive such information, advice, and referrals—that you should share your résumé with your letter recipient.

Time and again job searchers make the mistake of writing an approach letter but enclosing their résumé. Such ill-conceived actions generate contradictory messages. While they may produce an outstanding approach letter, they in effect kill it by attaching a résumé. The letter says they are only asking for information, advice, and referrals, but the enclosed résumé implies they are actually looking for a job from the letter recipient. Such a contradictory message communicates to the recipient that he or she is likely to be abused by what appears to be an unethical or dishonest job seeker. They are unethical or dishonest because they use the approach letter and the informational interview as pretexts for asking for a job. This puts the recipients on the spot and makes them feel uncomfortable.

You may want to write two different types of approach letters for different situations: referral and cold turkey. The **referral approach letter** is written to someone based on a referral or a connection with someone else. A friend or acquaintance, for example, recommends that you contact a particular individual for job search information and advice:

> Why don't you contact John Staples. He really knows what's going on. I'm sure he'd be happy to give you advice on what he knows about the pharmaceutical industry in this area. Tell him I recommended that you give him a call.

This type of referral is **the** basis for building and expanding networks for conducting informational interviews that eventually lead to job interviews and offers. It's the type of referral you want to elicit again and again in the process of expanding your job search network into the offices of potential employers. When you receive such a referral, you have one of two choices for developing the connection.

First, depending on the situation and the individual's position, you may want to immediately initiate the contact by telephone. The use of the telephone is efficient; it gets the job done quickly. However, it is not always the most effective way of initiating a contact. You may encounter voice mail; the individual may be very busy and thus unable to take your call, or he may be in the middle of some important business that should not be interrupted by someone like you. When you telephone a stranger, you may face immediate resistance to any attempt to use his valuable time or schedule an informational interview.

Second, you may want to write a referral approach letter. While not as efficient as a telephone call, this letter is likely to be more effective. It prepares the individual for your telephone call. Such a letter enables you to be in complete control of the one-way communication; you should be better able to craft an effective message that will lead to a productive telephone call and informational interview.

This type of approach letter should immediately open with a personal statement that nicely connects you to the reader via your referral and a bit of flattery. Start with something like this:

> John Staples suggested that I contact you regarding the local pharmaceutical industry. He said you know the business better than anyone else.

> When I spoke with Mary Thompson today, she highly recommended you as a source of information on the local pharmaceutical industry.

Such statements include two positives that should result in a favorable impression on the receiver: You've already been screened by the referral for making this contact, and this individual is recognized as an expert in the eyes of others who are important to him who, in turn, pass this recognition on to others.

The next two paragraphs should indicate your interests, motivations, and background in reference to the purpose of making this contact. It should clearly communicate your intentions for making this contact and for using the individual's time. You might say something like this:

> After several successful years in pharmaceutical sales and marketing in Boston, I've decided to relocate to the Midwest where I can be closer to my family. However, having moved to the East nearly 15 years ago, I've discovered I'm somewhat of a stranger to the industry in this area.

> I would very much appreciate any information and advice you might be able to share with me on the nature of the pharmaceutical industry in the greater Chicago Metro area. I have several questions I'm hoping to find answers to in the coming weeks. Perhaps, as John said, you could fill me in on the who, what, and where of the local industry.

Throughout this letter, as well as in your telephone conversation or in a face-to-face meeting, you should **never** indicate that you are looking for a job through this individual. You are only seeking information and advice. If this contact results in referrals that lead to job interviews and offers, that's great. But you are explicitly initiating this contact because you need more information and advice at this stage of your job search. This individual, in effect, becomes your personal advisor—not your future employer. Individuals who use the approach letter for the purpose of getting a job through the recipient abuse this form of communication. Their actions are exploitive, and they tend to become undesirable nuisances few people want to hire. Worse still, they give networking and informational interviewing bad names.

Whatever you do, make sure you are completely honest when you approach referral contacts for information and advice. You will get better cooperation and information as well as be seen as a thoughtful individual who should be promoted through referrals and networking. Therefore, the second and third paragraphs of your letter should indicate your true intentions in initiating this contact.

Your final paragraph should consist of an action statement which indicates what you will do next:

> I'll give you a call Tuesday afternoon to see if your schedule would permit some time to discuss my interests in the local pharmaceutical industry. I appreciate your time and look forward to talking with you in a few days.

You—not the letter recipient—must take follow-up action on this letter. You should never end such a letter with an action statement requesting the recipient to contact you (*"I look forward to hearing from you"* or *"Please give me a call if your schedule would permit us to meet"*). If you do, you will not receive a reply. As we will see in Chapter 8, it's incumbent upon you to further initiate the contact with a telephone call. Assuming you sent the letter by regular first-class mail, try to leave at least four days between when you mailed the letter and when you make the telephone call. If you use special next-day delivery services, make your call on the same delivery day, preferably between 2pm and 4pm.

This action statement prepares the contact for your telephone call and subsequent conversation or meeting. He or she will most likely give you some time. However, please note that this action statement is also a thoughtful conclusion that does not specify the nature of your future contact nor is it overly aggressive or presumptuous (*"I'll schedule a meeting"*). The open-ended statement *"to see if your schedule would permit some time"* could result in either a telephone interview or a face-to-face meeting. In many cases a telephone interview will suffice. The individual may have a limited amount of information that is best shared in a 5-10 minute telephone call. In other cases, a face-to-face half-hour to one-hour informational interview would be more appropriate. By choosing such a closing action statement, you leave the time, place, and medium of the interview open to discussion.

> **If you lack a referral, make a logical connection between you and the letter recipient in your opening paragraph. Make your connection as warm, personal, and professional as possible.**

The **cold-turkey approach letter** is written for the same purpose but without a personal contact. In this case you literally approach a stranger with no prior contacts. In contrast to the referral approach letter, in this situation you do not have instant credibility attendant with a personal connect. While cold-turkey contacts can be difficult to initiate, they can play an important role in your job search campaign.

Since you do not have a personal contact to introduce you to the letter recipient, you need to begin your letter with an appropriate "cold call" opener that logically connects you to the reader. Try to make your connection as warm, personal, and professional as possible. Avoid excessive flattery or boastful statements that are likely to make your motives suspect and thus turn off the reader. It's always helpful to inject in this letter a personal observation that gently strokes the ego of the reader. If, for example, you read a newspaper article about the individual's work, or if he or she recently received an award or promotion, you might introduce yourself in this letter in any of the following ways:

> I read with great interest about your work with _____.
> Congratulations on a job well done. During the past twelve years I've been involved in similar work.

> Congratulations on receiving the annual community award. Your efforts have certainly helped revitalize our downtown area. My interests in urban development began nearly ten years ago when I was studying urban planning at St. Louis University.

> Congratulations on your recent promotion to Vice President of Allied Materials. I've been one of your admirers for the past five years, following your many community and professional activities. Your work in expanding Allied Materials' markets to Japan and China especially interests me because of my previous work in Asia.

Other openers might begin with some of the following lead-in phrases which help connect you to the reader:

> I am writing to you because of your position as . . .

> Because of your experience in . . .

> We have a common interest in . . .

> Since we are both alumni of Texas A&M, I thought . . .

> As a fellow member of Alpha Chi Omega sorority, I wanted to congratulate you on your recent election to . . .

Whatever opener you choose, make sure you focus on making a **logical connection** that is both personal and professional. Inject some personality in this letter. After all, you want this stranger to take an immediate interest in you. Try to communicate that you are a likable, enthusiastic, honest, and competent person worth talking to or even meeting. The very first sentence should grab the reader's attention.

A strong opener in a cold-turkey approach letter can be nearly as effective as the personal contact opener in the referral approach letter.

The remaining paragraphs of the cold-turkey referral letter will be structured similarly to the referral approach letter—indicate your interests, motivations, and background in reference to your purpose in making this contact. Clearly communicate your intentions for making this contact and for using the individual's time. Again, be perfectly honest and tactful in what you say, but avoid making honest but stupid statements, such as *"I really don't know what's going to happen to me in the next three months."* Be sure to close with an indication of action—you will call on a particular date to see if the person's schedule would permit some time to discuss your interests.

If you incorporate these two types of approach letters in your job search, you will quickly discover they are the most powerful forms of communication in your job search arsenal. They must be written and targeted toward individuals who have information, advice, and referrals relevant to your job search interests. They are the bricks and mortar for building networks that generate informational interviews that lead to job interviews and offers. Résumés and telephone calls are no substitute for these referral letters. A résumé **never** accompanies these letters, and a telephone call only follows **after** the recipient has received and read your approach letter. If you write these letters according to our suggested structure and content and follow-up with the telephone call, you will receive a great deal of useful job search information, advice, and referrals. You will learn about the structure of the job market, identify key players who can help you, and inject a healthy dose of reality into a job search that may otherwise be guided by myths and wishful thinking.

If for any reason you still feel compelled to sneak a résumé in the envelope with one of these approach letters, you will quickly discover few recipients want to see or talk with you. The enclosed résumé immediately transforms what was potentially an effective approach letter into an ineffective cover letter for a job application—something that is inappropriate in this situation. As we've already seen, an effective cover letter has a different purpose as well as follows other writing, distribution, and follow-up principles.

Thank-You Letters

Thank-you letters are some of the most effective communications in a job search. They demonstrate an important **social grace** that says something about you as an individual—your personality and how you probably relate to others. They communicate one of the most important characteristics sought in potential employees—**thoughtfulness**.

Better still, since few individuals write thank-you letters, those who do write them are **remembered** by letter recipients. And one thing you definitely want to happen again and again during your job search is to be remembered by individuals who can provide you with useful information, advice, and referrals as well as invite you to job interviews and extend to you job offers. Being remembered as a thoughtful person with the proper social graces will give you an edge over many other job seekers who fail to write thank-you letters. Whatever you do, make sure you regularly send thank-you letters in response to individuals who assist you in your job search.

Many job seekers discover the most important letters they ever wrote were thank-you letters. These letters can have several positive outcomes:

- **Contacts turn into more contacts and job interviews:** A job seeker sends a thank-you letter to someone who recommended they contact a former college roommate; impressed with the thoughtfulness of the job seeker and feeling somewhat responsible for helping her make the right contacts, the individual continues providing additional referrals, which eventually lead to two job interviews.

- **Job interview turns into a job offer:** A job seeker completes a job interview. Within 24-hours he writes a nice thank-you in which he expresses his gratitude for having an opportunity to interview for the position as well as reiterates his interest in working for the employer. This individual is subsequently offered the job. The employer later tells him it was his thoughtful thank-you letter that gave him the edge over two other equally qualified candidates who never bothered to follow-up the interview.

- **A job rejection later turns into a job offer:** After interviewing for a position, a job seeker receives a standard rejection letter from an employer indicating the job was offered to another individual. Rather than get angry and end communications with the employer, the job seeker sends a nice thank-you letter in which she notes her disappointment in not being selected and then thanks him for the opportunity to interview for the position. She also reiterates her continuing interest in working for the organization. The employer remembers this individual. Rather than let her get away, he decides to create a new position for her.

- **A job offer turns into an immediate positive relationship:** Upon receiving a job offer, the new employee sends a nice thank-you letter in which he expresses his enthusiasm in joining the company as well as stresses his appreciation for the confidence expressed in him by the employer. He also reassures the employer that he will be as productive as expected. This letter is well received by the employer who is looking forward to working closely with such a thoughtful new employee. Indeed, he becomes a mentor and sponsor who immediately gives the employee some plum assignments that help him fast-track his career within the organization.

- **Termination results in strong recommendations and a future job offer:** An employee, seeking to advance her career with a larger organization, receives a job offer from a competing firm. In submitting her formal letter of resignation, she also sends a personal thank-you letter to her former employer. She sincerely expresses her gratitude for having the opportunity work with him and attributes much of her success to his mentoring. This letter further confirms his conclusion about this former employee—he's loosing a valuable asset. While he can not offer her a similar or better career opportunity in this organization, he will keep her in mind if things change. And things do change two years later when he makes a major career move to a much larger organization. One of the first things he does as Vice-President is to begin shaping his own personal staff. He immediately contacts her to see if she would be interested in working with him. She's interested and soon joins her former employer in making another major career move.

In these cases it was the job seekers' thank-you letters, rather than their cover letters and résumés, that got them job interviews and offers.

As indicated in the above scenarios, thank-you letters should be written in the following situations:

- **After receiving information, advice, or a referral from a contact:** You should always express your gratitude in writing to individuals who provide you with job search assistance. Not only is this a nice thing to do, it also is functional for a successful job search. Individuals who feel they are appreciated will most likely remember you and be willing to further assist you with your job search and recommend you to others.

- **Immediately after interviewing for a job:** Whether it be a telephone or face-to-face interview, always write a nice thank-you letter within twelve hours of completing the interview. This letter should express your gratitude for having an opportunity to interview for the job. Be sure to reiterate your interest in the job and stress your possible contributions to the employer's operations. The letter should emphasize your major strengths in relationship to the employer's needs. All other things being equal, this letter may give you an "extra edge" over other candidates. It may well prove to be your most effective letter in your entire job search!

- **Withdrawing from further consideration:** At some point during the recruitment process, you may decide to withdraw from further consideration. Perhaps you decided to take another job, you're now more satisfied with your present job, or the position no longer interests you. For whatever reason, you should write a short thank-you letter in which you withdraw from consideration. Explain in positive terms why you are no longer interested in pursuing an application with the organization. Thank them for their time and consideration.

- **After receiving a rejection:** Even if you receive a rejection, it's a good idea to write a thank-you letter. How many employers ever receive such a letter from what ostensibly should be a disappointed job seeker? This unique letter is likely to be remembered—which is what you want to accomplish in this situation. Being remembered may result in referrals to other employers or perhaps a job interview and offer at some later date.

- **After receiving a job offer:** However well they think they hire, employers still are uncertain about the outcome of their hiring decisions until new employees perform in their organization. Why not put their initial anxieties at ease and get off on the right foot by writing a nice thank-you letter? In this letter express your appreciation for having received the confidence and trust of the employer. Reiterate what you told the employer during the job interview(s) about your goals and expected performance. Conclude with a reaffirmation of your starting date as well as a statement about how much you look forward to becoming a productive member of the team. Such a thoughtful letter will be well received by the employer. It could well accelerate your progress within the organization beyond the norm.

- **Upon leaving a job:** Whether you leave your job voluntarily or are forced by circumstances to terminate, try to leave a positive part of you behind by writing a thank-you letter. Burning bridges behind you through face-to-face confrontation or a vindictive, get-even letter may later catch up with you, especially if you anger someone in the process who may later be in a position to affect your career. If you quit to take a job with another organization, thank your employer for the time you spent with the organization and the opportunities given to you to acquire valuable experience and skills. If you terminated under difficult circumstances—organizational cutbacks or a nasty firing—try to leave on as positive a note as possible. Employers in such situations would rather have you out of sight and mind. Assure them there are no hard feelings, and you wish them the best as you would hope they would wish you the same. Stress the positives of your relationship with both the employer and the organization. Remember, your future employer may call your previous employer for information on your past performance. If you leave a stressful situation on a positive note, chances are your previous employer will give you the benefit of the doubt and stress only your positives to others. He may even commit a few "sins of omission" that only you and he know about: *"She really worked well with her co-workers and was one of our best analysts"* does not tell the whole story which may be that you couldn't get along with your boss, and vice versa. After having made peace with each other through the medium of the thank-you letter, what would your former employer have to gain by telling the whole story to others about your work with him? Your thank-you letter should at least neutralize the situation and at best turn a negative situation into a positive for your career. Indeed, he may well become one of your supporters—for other jobs with other employers, that is!

Examples of each type of letter, written according to our principles of effective thank-you letters, appear at the end of this chapter and are identified accordingly.

Thank-you letters should always be written in a timely manner. Make it a practice to sit down and write these letters within twelve hours of the situation that prompts this letter. It should be mailed immediately so that it reaches the recipient within three to four days. If you wait longer, the letter will have less impact on the situation. Indeed, in the case of the interview thank-you letter, if an employer is making a final hiring decision among three candidates, your letter should arrive as soon as possible to have a chance to affect the outcome.

Whether you handwrite or type this letter may not make a great deal of difference in terms of outcomes, but your choice says something about your professional style and mentality. Many people claim handwritten thank-you letters are more powerful than typed letters. We doubt such claims and have yet to see any credible data on the subject other than personal preferences and questionable logic. It is true that handwritten thank-you letters communicate a certain personal element that cannot be expressed in typewritten letters. If you choose to handwrite this letter, make sure you have attractive handwriting. Your handwriting form and style could be a negative.

> ❑ **Thank-you letters communicate one of the most important characteristics sought in potential employees—thoughtfulness.**
>
> ❑ **You may discover your thank-you letters have the greatest impact of any job search communication.**
>
> ❑ **Make a practice of writing a thank-you letter within 12-hours of the situation that prompted the letter.**
>
> ❑ **Type rather than handwrite your thank-you letters. Remember, this is business communication that should express your best professional effort.**

The problem with handwritten letters is that they can express a certain nonprofessional, amateurish style. They also may raise questions about your motivations and manipulative style. They turn off some readers who expect a business letter, rather than an expression of social graces, in reference to a business situation. Furthermore, some readers may consider the handwritten letter an attempt at psychological manipulation—they know what you're trying to do by handwriting a letter. That's what real estate and car salespeople are taught to do in their training seminars!

When in doubt, it's best to type this letter in a neat, clean, and professional manner. If typewritten, such a personal letter also will express your professional style and respond to the expectations appropriate for the situation. It tells the reader that you know proper business etiquette, you know this is a business situation, you are equipped to respond, and you attempt to demonstrate your best professional effort.

Résumé Letters

A résumé letter is a special type of approach letter that substitutes for a formal résumé. Merging the cover letter and résumé into a single document, this type of letter is written when it is appropriate to target your qualifications in a format other than a separate cover letter and résumé. It's most often used to approach employers with information on your experience and skills in the hope that they will have vacancies for someone with your qualifications.

Since it outlines your experience and skills, the résumé letter is designed to get job interviews with employers. It, in effect, asks for a job interview rather than information, advice, or referrals for expanding your job search.

Similar to the cold-turkey approach letter, the résumé letter should open with a logical connection between you and the employer. The second paragraph, however, is what defines this as a résumé letter. This paragraph should summarize your major experience and skills in relation to the employer's needs. In fact, you may want to take this section directly from the "Areas of Effectiveness," "Experience," or "Work History" section appearing on your résumé. For ease of reading, it's best to bullet each item, preferably including three to five items similar to the examples found at the end of this chapter. The final paragraph should call for action—you taking the initiative to call the recipient at a specific time for the purpose of scheduling a possible interview.

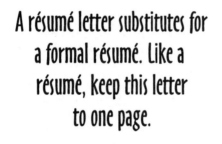

A résumé letter substitutes for a formal résumé. Like a résumé, keep this letter to one page.

You should try to keep this letter to a single page. Remember, it is neither a cover letter nor a résumé, but a combination of both which has a specific purpose—you are trying to invite yourself to a job interview. Since this type of letter tends to put employers on the spot—here's another "cold-caller"—it will probably generate few positive responses and numerous rejections. However well written this letter may be, few employers are prepared to give job interviews based on such a letter. Chances are most employers will not have vacancies available at the time you send this letter. What they may be able to do is give you referrals to other employers who may have vacancies—but only if you follow-up this letter with a phone call. In the end, your résumé letter may become an important prospecting letter for uncovering job leads.

COVER LETTER
Response to Advertised Position

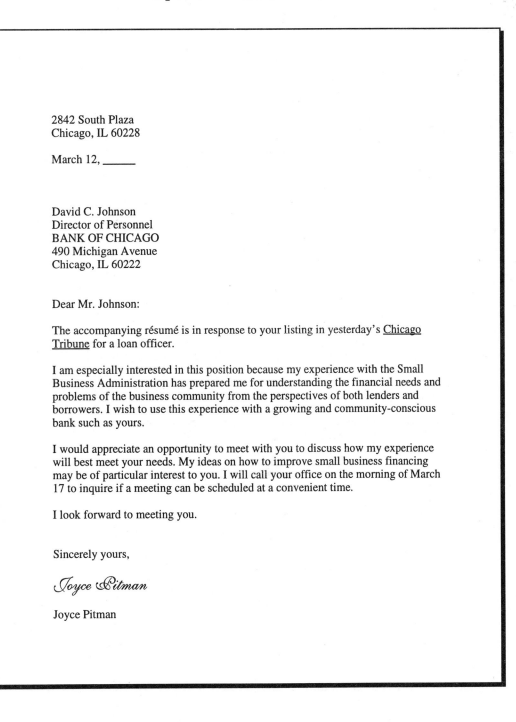

2842 South Plaza
Chicago, IL 60228

March 12, _____

David C. Johnson
Director of Personnel
BANK OF CHICAGO
490 Michigan Avenue
Chicago, IL 60222

Dear Mr. Johnson:

The accompanying résumé is in response to your listing in yesterday's <u>Chicago Tribune</u> for a loan officer.

I am especially interested in this position because my experience with the Small Business Administration has prepared me for understanding the financial needs and problems of the business community from the perspectives of both lenders and borrowers. I wish to use this experience with a growing and community-conscious bank such as yours.

I would appreciate an opportunity to meet with you to discuss how my experience will best meet your needs. My ideas on how to improve small business financing may be of particular interest to you. I will call your office on the morning of March 17 to inquire if a meeting can be scheduled at a convenient time.

I look forward to meeting you.

Sincerely yours,

Joyce Pitman

Joyce Pitman

COVER LETTER
Referral

2237 South Olby Road
Sacramento, CA 97342

July 17, _____

David Myers
Vice President
FULTON ENGINEERING CORPORATION
1254 Madison Street
Sacramento, CA 97340

Dear Mr. Myers:

John Bird, the Director of Data Systems at Ottings Engineering Company, informed me that you are looking for someone to direct your new management information system.

I enclose my résumé for your consideration. During the past 10 years I have developed and supervised a variety of systems. I have worked at both the operational and managerial levels and know how to develop systems appropriate for different types of organizations.

I would appreciate an opportunity to visit with you and examine your operations. Perhaps I could provide you with a needs assessment prior to an interview. I will call you next week to make arrangements for a visit.

I look forward to speaking with you next week.

Sincerely,

Gary S. Platt

Gary S. Platt

APPROACH LETTER
Referral

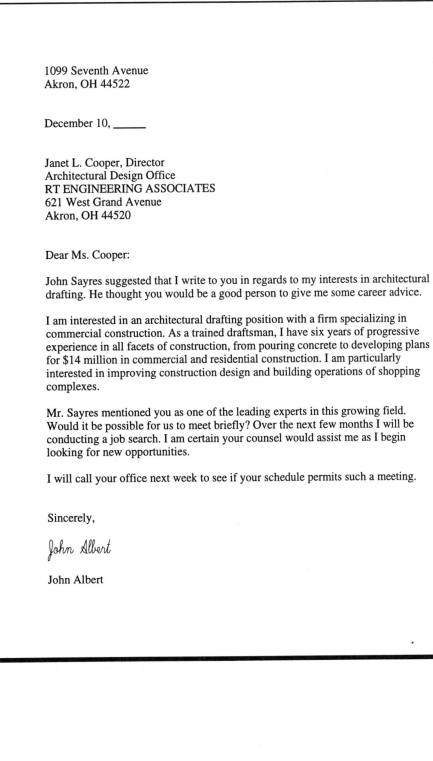

1099 Seventh Avenue
Akron, OH 44522

December 10, _____

Janet L. Cooper, Director
Architectural Design Office
RT ENGINEERING ASSOCIATES
621 West Grand Avenue
Akron, OH 44520

Dear Ms. Cooper:

John Sayres suggested that I write to you in regards to my interests in architectural drafting. He thought you would be a good person to give me some career advice.

I am interested in an architectural drafting position with a firm specializing in commercial construction. As a trained draftsman, I have six years of progressive experience in all facets of construction, from pouring concrete to developing plans for $14 million in commercial and residential construction. I am particularly interested in improving construction design and building operations of shopping complexes.

Mr. Sayres mentioned you as one of the leading experts in this growing field. Would it be possible for us to meet briefly? Over the next few months I will be conducting a job search. I am certain your counsel would assist me as I begin looking for new opportunities.

I will call your office next week to see if your schedule permits such a meeting.

Sincerely,

John Albert

John Albert

APPROACH LETTER
Cold Turkey

2189 West Church Street
New York, NY 10011

May 3, _____

Patricia Dotson, Director
NORTHEAST ASSOCIATION
  FOR THE ELDERLY
9930 Jefferson Street
New York, NY 10013

Dear Ms. Dotson:

I have been impressed with your work with the elderly. Your organization takes a community perspective in trying to integrate the concerns of the elderly with those of other community groups. Perhaps other organizations will soon follow your lead.

I am anxious to meet you and learn more about your work. My background with the city Volunteer Services Program involved frequent contact with elderly volunteers. From this experience I decided I preferred working primarily with the elderly.

However, before I pursue my interest further, I need to talk to people with experience in gerontology. In particular, I would like to know more about careers with the elderly as well as how my background might best be used in the field of gerontology.

In am hoping you can assist me in this matter. I would like to meet with you briefly to discuss several of my concerns. I will call next week to see if your schedule permits such a meeting.

I look forward to meeting you.

Sincerely,

Carol Timms

Carol Timms

THANK-YOU LETTER
Referral

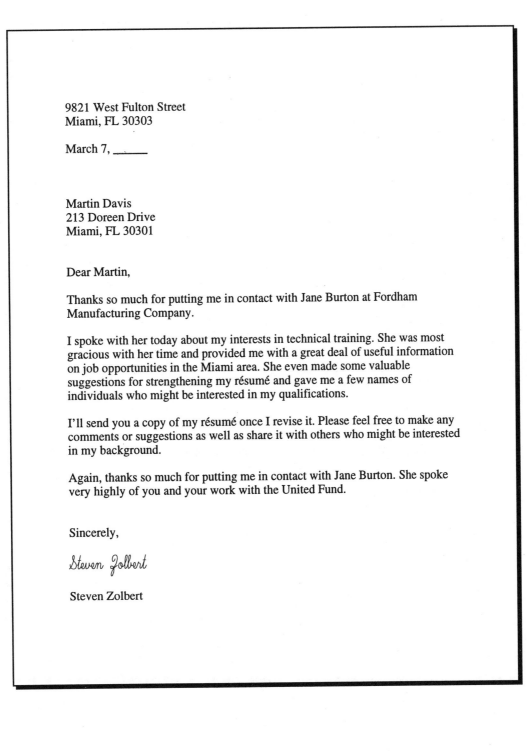

9821 West Fulton Street
Miami, FL 30303

March 7, _____

Martin Davis
213 Doreen Drive
Miami, FL 30301

Dear Martin,

Thanks so much for putting me in contact with Jane Burton at Fordham
Manufacturing Company.

I spoke with her today about my interests in technical training. She was most
gracious with her time and provided me with a great deal of useful information
on job opportunities in the Miami area. She even made some valuable
suggestions for strengthening my résumé and gave me a few names of
individuals who might be interested in my qualifications.

I'll send you a copy of my résumé once I revise it. Please feel free to make any
comments or suggestions as well as share it with others who might be interested
in my background.

Again, thanks so much for putting me in contact with Jane Burton. She spoke
very highly of you and your work with the United Fund.

Sincerely,

Steven Zolbert

Steven Zolbert

THANK-YOU LETTER
After Informational Interview

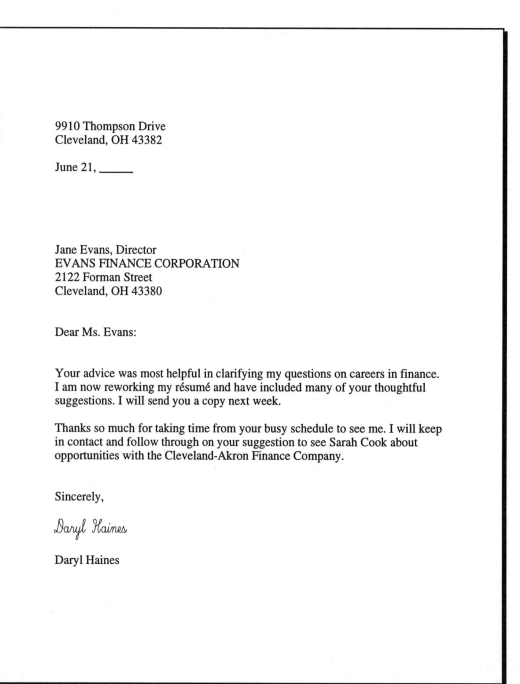

9910 Thompson Drive
Cleveland, OH 43382

June 21, _____

Jane Evans, Director
EVANS FINANCE CORPORATION
2122 Forman Street
Cleveland, OH 43380

Dear Ms. Evans:

Your advice was most helpful in clarifying my questions on careers in finance.
I am now reworking my résumé and have included many of your thoughtful
suggestions. I will send you a copy next week.

Thanks so much for taking time from your busy schedule to see me. I will keep
in contact and follow through on your suggestion to see Sarah Cook about
opportunities with the Cleveland-Akron Finance Company.

Sincerely,

Daryl Haines

Daryl Haines

THANK-YOU LETTER
Post Job Interview

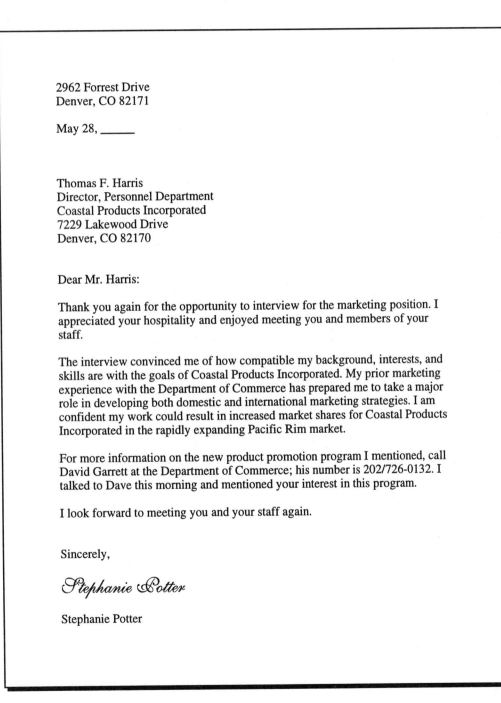

2962 Forrest Drive
Denver, CO 82171

May 28, _____

Thomas F. Harris
Director, Personnel Department
Coastal Products Incorporated
7229 Lakewood Drive
Denver, CO 82170

Dear Mr. Harris:

Thank you again for the opportunity to interview for the marketing position. I appreciated your hospitality and enjoyed meeting you and members of your staff.

The interview convinced me of how compatible my background, interests, and skills are with the goals of Coastal Products Incorporated. My prior marketing experience with the Department of Commerce has prepared me to take a major role in developing both domestic and international marketing strategies. I am confident my work could result in increased market shares for Coastal Products Incorporated in the rapidly expanding Pacific Rim market.

For more information on the new product promotion program I mentioned, call David Garrett at the Department of Commerce; his number is 202/726-0132. I talked to Dave this morning and mentioned your interest in this program.

I look forward to meeting you and your staff again.

Sincerely,

Stephanie Potter

Stephanie Potter

THANK-YOU LETTER
Responding to Rejection

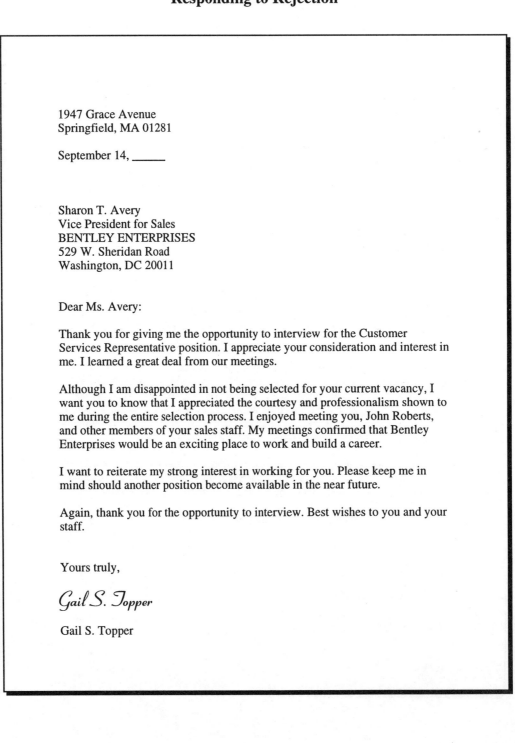

1947 Grace Avenue
Springfield, MA 01281

September 14, _____

Sharon T. Avery
Vice President for Sales
BENTLEY ENTERPRISES
529 W. Sheridan Road
Washington, DC 20011

Dear Ms. Avery:

Thank you for giving me the opportunity to interview for the Customer
Services Representative position. I appreciate your consideration and interest in
me. I learned a great deal from our meetings.

Although I am disappointed in not being selected for your current vacancy, I
want you to know that I appreciated the courtesy and professionalism shown to
me during the entire selection process. I enjoyed meeting you, John Roberts,
and other members of your sales staff. My meetings confirmed that Bentley
Enterprises would be an exciting place to work and build a career.

I want to reiterate my strong interest in working for you. Please keep me in
mind should another position become available in the near future.

Again, thank you for the opportunity to interview. Best wishes to you and your
staff.

Yours truly,

Gail S. Topper

Gail S. Topper

THANK-YOU LETTER
Withdrawing From Consideration

733 Main Street
Williamsburg, VA 23512

December 1, _____

Dr. Thomas C. Bostelli, President
Northern States University
2500 University Drive
Greenfield, MA 03241

Dear Dr. Bostelli:

It was indeed a pleasure meeting with you and your staff last week to discuss your need for a Director of Public and Government Relations. Our time together was most enjoyable and informative.

As I discussed with you during our meetings, I believe one purpose of preliminary interviews is to explore areas of mutual interest and to assess the fit between the individual and the position. After careful consideration, I have decided to withdraw from consideration for the position.

My decision is based upon several factors. First, the emphasis on fund raising is certainly needed, but I would prefer more balance in my work activities. Second, the position would require more travel than I am willing to accept with my other responsibilities. Third, professional opportunities for my husband would be very limited in northwest Massachusetts.

I want to thank you for interviewing me and giving me the opportunity to learn about your needs. You have a fine staff and faculty, and I would have enjoyed working with them.

Best wishes in your search.

Sincerely,

Janet L. Lawson

Janet L. Lawson

THANK-YOU LETTER
Accepting Job Offer

7694 James Courts
San Francisco, CA 94826

June 7, _____

Judith Greene
Vice President
WEST COAST AIRLINES
2400 Van Ness
San Francisco, CA 94829

Dear Ms. Greene:

I am pleased to accept your offer, and I am looking forward to joining you and your staff next month.

The customer relations position is ideally suited to my background and interests. I assure you I will give you my best effort in making this an effective position within your company.

I understand I will begin work on July 1. If, in the meantime, I need to complete any paper work or take care of any other matters, please contact me at 377-4029.

I enjoyed meeting with you and your staff and appreciated the professional manner in which the hiring was conducted.

Sincerely,

Joan Kitner

Joan Kitner

THANK-YOU LETTER
Terminating Employment

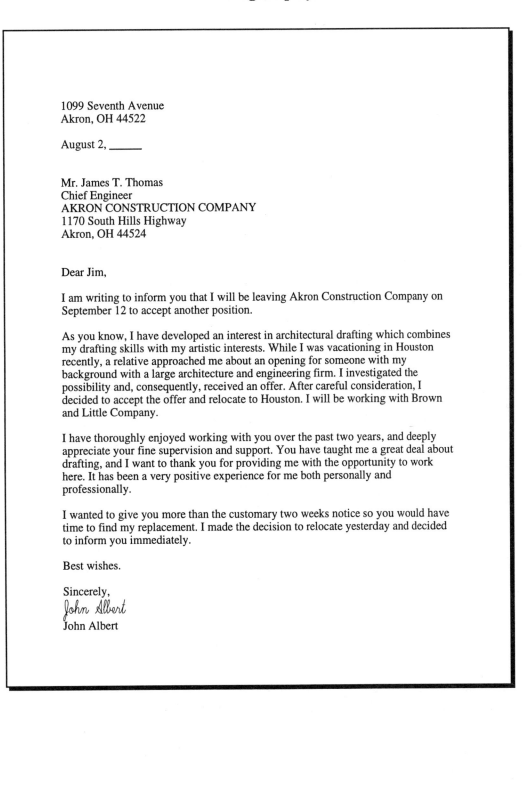

1099 Seventh Avenue
Akron, OH 44522

August 2, _____

Mr. James T. Thomas
Chief Engineer
AKRON CONSTRUCTION COMPANY
1170 South Hills Highway
Akron, OH 44524

Dear Jim,

I am writing to inform you that I will be leaving Akron Construction Company on September 12 to accept another position.

As you know, I have developed an interest in architectural drafting which combines my drafting skills with my artistic interests. While I was vacationing in Houston recently, a relative approached me about an opening for someone with my background with a large architecture and engineering firm. I investigated the possibility and, consequently, received an offer. After careful consideration, I decided to accept the offer and relocate to Houston. I will be working with Brown and Little Company.

I have thoroughly enjoyed working with you over the past two years, and deeply appreciate your fine supervision and support. You have taught me a great deal about drafting, and I want to thank you for providing me with the opportunity to work here. It has been a very positive experience for me both personally and professionally.

I wanted to give you more than the customary two weeks notice so you would have time to find my replacement. I made the decision to relocate yesterday and decided to inform you immediately.

Best wishes.

Sincerely,

John Albert

John Albert

RÉSUMÉ LETTER

773 Main Street
Williamsburg, VA 23572

November 12, _____

Barbara Thompson, President
SRM ASSOCIATES
421 91st Street
New York, NY 11910

Dear Ms. Thompson:

I just completed reading the article in <u>Business Today</u> on SRM Associates. Your innovative approach to recruiting minorities is of particular interest to me because of my background in public relations and minority recruitment.

I am interested in learning more about your work as well as the possibilities of joining your firm. My qualifications include:

- research and writing on minority recruitment and medical education
- secured funding and administered $845,000 minority representation program
- published several professional articles and reports on creative writing, education, and minorities
- organized and led public relations, press, and minority conferences
- M.A. in Journalism and B.A. in English

I will be in New York City during the week of December 10. Perhaps your schedule would permit us to meet briefly to discuss our mutual interests. I will call your office next week to see if such a meeting can be arranged.

I appreciate your consideration.

Sincerely yours,

Michele R. Folger

Michele R. Folger

RÉSUMÉ LETTER

4921 Tyler Drive
Washington, DC 20011

March 15, _____

Doris Stevens
STR CORPORATION
179 South Trail
Rockville, MD 21101

Dear Ms. Stevens:

STR Corporation is one of the most dynamic computer companies in the nation. Its model employee training and development program makes it the type of organization I am interested in joining.

I am seeking a training position with a computer firm which would use my administrative, communication, and planning abilities to develop effective training and counseling programs. My experience includes:

Administration: Supervised instructors and counselors. Coordinated job vacancy and training information for businesses and schools.

Communication: Conducted over 100 workshops on interpersonal skills, stress management, and career planning. Frequent guest speaker to various agencies and private firms. Experienced writer of training manuals and public relations materials.

Planning: Planned and developed counseling programs for over 5,000 employees. Reorganized interviewing and screening processes and developed program of individualized and group counseling.

I am also completing my Ph.D. in industrial psychology with an emphasis on developing training and counseling programs for technical personnel.

Could we meet to discuss your program as well as how my experience might relate to your needs? I will call your office on Tuesday morning, March 23, to arrange a convenient time.

I especially want to show you a model employee counseling and career development program I recently developed. Perhaps you may find it useful for your work with STR.

Sincerely,

James C. Astor

James C. Astor

4

Form, Structure, and Design

Effective letter writing is hard yet rewarding work. It involves much more than just sticking a piece of paper in the typewriter or turning on a wordprocessor, pounding out a few sentences and paragraphs, and depositing the product in a mail box or transmitting it electronically. Above all, it requires knowledge about the elements of effective communication and the reading behavior of busy letter recipients. If you want to write dynamite cover letters, you must incorporate the principles of good form, structure, and design in your letter writing activities.

Effective Communication

Most individuals receiving your letters are busy people. Indeed, many hiring officials are inundated with letters and résumés. Some receive over 500 letters a week, but they only have an hour or less a day, interspersed with numerous telephone calls and meetings, to read all their mail, including an increasing volume of e-mail.

What would you do if you were faced with such volume of written communication? Busy people simply don't have the time nor motivation to read every word on the page and then sit back and contemplate what they should do next in response to each letter. No wonder many letter writers never receive

64

responses to their job search letters!

Most high-volume letter recipients find shortcuts that help them dispose of each letter within a few seconds (5-10 seconds) so they will have time (30-60 seconds) to read only the most interesting ones. Such seemingly superficial elements as the general "look" of the envelope and letter—its form, structure, layout—color and weight of paper, type style, salutation, and signature are the first things readers see. How these elements come together to communicate a professional image is important in determining whether or not your reader decides to discard your letter or continue reading for its content.

The old adage that *"you never have a second chance to make a good first impression"* applies equally to job search letters as it does to individuals invited to job interviews. Whatever you do, make sure all elements in your letter make a good first impression so your letter will receive the attention its contents require.

If you want your letters to be most effective—read and responded to—you need to make several important decisions concerning form, content, and distribution. Going beyond standard formats and models of so-called "good letters," you must be creative and thoughtful in planning and organizing your message. You must develop an appropriate form and style, structure appealing content, make important production and distribution decisions, and follow-up on the results of your communication. These are important and time consuming decisions. Failure to deal with any one of them will most likely result in ineffective job search communication. You will have difficulty communicating your qualifications to employers.

> **Your letter is likely to be received by someone who only has a few seconds to read it. Therefore, it must make a first good impression.**

Like other types of letters, job search letters should follow certain principles of effective form, structure, and design. While they say nothing about content or the details of your message, these letter writing elements nonetheless help communicate your message to the reader. Without strong form, structure, and design, your letters may become uninviting to the reader. Consider, for example, the hiring official who must review hundreds of letters and résumés each week. The most appealing letters exhibit strong elements of form, structure, and design. Essentially cosmetic in nature, these elements are the first ones communicated to the reader. They determine whether or not the reader will read the letter. If you neglect these elements, your letters may never pass the initial five second test of busy people—does it look interesting enough to invest the next minute of my time reading it?

Form and Structure

What form should you use? Is there one best way to structure the letter? What about my writing style? These questions frequently arise during the initial stages of learning how to write effective correspondence. And the answers to these questions continue to change depending on the goal of your writing and intended audience.

There is no one best form or style to use in letter writing. Instead, there are many alternatives to choose from, plus a great deal of flexibility permitted in being different, unique, and unusual. The business world tends to encourage flexibility and experimentation in most forms of communication. However, this should not be taken as a license to do anything you want to do. You must know your purpose, your audience, and your alternative forms and styles before choosing one that is most appropriate for your particular situation.

Let's examine some standard alternative formats. Most letters include the following elements in their layout:

1. Heading
2. Date line
3. Inside address
4. Salutation or greeting
5. Body of letter
6. Closing
7. Signature lines
8. Identification initials
9. Enclosures
10. Copy reference
11. Postscript (P.S.)

The first seven elements are required for all business letters. The last four elements are optional depending on your particular situation; they seldom appear on job search letters. Each element should be laid out in the sequence as outlined on page 67. The particular style of the layout can vary. We'll discuss style variations when we examine typing styles.

STANDARD LETTER ELEMENTS

① heading

② date line

inside address ③

salutation ④

body ⑤

⑥ closing

⑦ signature line

identification initials ⑧

enclosures ⑨

copy reference ⑩

postscript ⑪

The structure of each letter element follows strict rules, although some variation is permitted in a few cases. When in doubt about a particular rule or its variation, make a decision based upon your understanding of the purpose of the letter—communicate your best professional image with impact. Your common sense may dictate the best course to take.

1. Heading

Letters have two types of headings. The first is **letterhead** or a heading pre-printed on company stationery or with an individual's name and address. When writing job search letters, it is inappropriate to use your present employer's letterhead. Doing so communicates the wrong message to a potential future employer—you abuse employers' resources. In addition, potential employers may call you at work, which could prove embarrassing if you are trying to keep your job search secret. Personal letterhead stationery can look very professional, especially if it is printed with raised letters on 20 lb. bond white, off white, or light grey paper. However, it is not necessary to go to the expense of personalized stationery. It may look a bit extravagant to some employers. On the other hand, if you produce your letters using a standard wordprocessing program and a laser printer, you should be able to easily design your own attractive letterhead.

The second type of heading is the **standard plain letter form**. Since nothing is preprinted on the stationery, the writer supplies his or her contact information beginning near the top-right-center of the stationery. The contact information includes only the address immediately followed by a date line:

973 W. 191st Street
Kent, WA 93201

January 27, 1999

2. Date Line

The date line comes immediately after the heading. It should appear in one of two forms: month-day-year or day-month-year:

September 11, 1999   11 September 1999

The month-day-year form is used most commonly in the United States. The day-month-year is the standard form used in international communications.

Always write the date in full. Do not abbreviate. It's best to leave one space between the heading and the date line as outlined in our example above and on the previous page.

3. Inside Address

The inside address consists of the title, name, position, company, and address of the organization receiving your letter. The following rules should be followed:

TITLE: Always address your letter recipient by his or her proper gender or professional title. You have several alternatives depending on whom you are writing to:

Mr.	male
Mrs.	married female
Miss	unmarried female
Ms.	female if unsure of marital status
Messrs.*	more than one male
Mesdames*	more than one married female
Misses*	more than one unmarried female
Dr.	a Doctor of Medicine (M.D.)
	or
	Doctor of Philosophy (Ph.D.)

* Correct form, but seldom used.

NAME: Always try to address your letter to a specific person by name. Write the name in full—no nicknames, shortened forms, or abbreviations other than the middle initial or preferred usage by the individuals. "Dick" should be "Richard"; "Bob" should be "Robert"; "Jim" and "Jimmy" should be "James."

POSITION:	This is normally one's job title within the organization, such as Chairman, President, Chief of Personnel, Division Head.
COMPANY:	Complete name of the organization, including any subdivision such as departments, sections, and offices.
ADDRESS:	Street, post office box, city, state, zip code.

The principles of a proper inside address are illustrated in this example:

> Mr. James L. Tone
> Chairman of the Board
> Renkel Industries, Inc.
> 462 Fairfax Street
> San Francisco, CA 92101

4. Salutation

The salutation or greeting should consist of the greeting "Dear" followed by the proper gender or professional title and surname of the individual. Unless you are a close friend, never address the individual by a first name. Such a familial greeting is inappropriate for job search letters. A colon—not a comma—always follows the individual's last name:

> Dear Ms. Stevens:

In most cases you will have a name to which to address your letter or you can easily find the name by calling an organization and asking *"To whom should I send my letter?"* However, sometimes you will respond to a classified ad or job vacancy announcement which does not provide a name. The same is true if you broadcast letters to hundreds of anonymous employers. In these cases you should select one of the following alternatives:

- **Omit the salutation altogether.** This is our preference since the employer didn't bother to identify to whom the letter should be addressed. Don't worry, your letter will be delivered to the right person since you already have a title or department identified in your address.

Omitting the salutation avoids the problem of addressing a gender-sensitive person with the wrong title.

- **Try to neutralize a gender title by using**

> Dear Sir or Madam:
> Dear Sir/Madam:

However awkward, these are generally acceptable ways of addressing anonymous readers. Avoid addressing your reader as "Dear Gentleperson," "Dear Gentlepeople," "Dear Person," "Dear Sir," "Dear Ladies and Gentlemen," "Dear Future Employer," "Dear Friend," "Dear Company," "Dear Personnel Department," or "To Whom It May Concern." While they may appear more "correct" than the above titles, they're silly, insensitive, or presumptuous. If you can't do better than our examples, proceed to the body of the letter minus the salutation.

- **Use an attention line or a subject line.** Attention lines are used for quickly routing a letter to the proper reader. Subject lines are used for quick reference, routing, and filing purposes. You can use either in combination with a salutation—both before and after—or as a substitute for a salutation. In combination, these lines would appear as follows:

> Department of Personnel
> XYZ Corporation
> 1234 Mount Pleasant
> Chicago, IL 60000
>
> ATTENTION: Director of Personnel
>
> Dear Director:
>
> SUBJECT: Area manager position

You can also use them alone or as a substitute for the traditional salutation. Instead of beginning with "Dear Sir/Madam," for example, start with "ATTENTION: Director of Personnel" or "SUBJECT: Area manager position." Attention and subject lines are especially helpful in routing letters within large organizations that recruit for numerous positions.

5. Body and Continuation Pages

The body of your letter normally should be organized so it fits on a single page. The following structural rules should be observed with writing this section:

- **Subdivide the letter into two to four paragraphs:** A single paragraph says too little and more than four paragraphs begins to include too many ideas. Keep the letter simple and to the point by only addressing three or four points.

- **Avoid lengthy paragraphs of more than five lines:** Long paragraphs look uninviting, are hard to follow, and are often cluttered with too many ideas. Five line paragraphs that include two to three sentences per paragraph will serve you well.

- **Keep most sentences to 25 words or fewer.** Similar to long para-graphs, long sentences are uninviting and are often hard to follow. Keep your sentences simple and to the point.

If you must go beyond one page, your continuation pages should be referenced in some manner. Make sure your continuation pages are always connected with the first page so it cannot be confused with other letters. The most formal and complete continuation page form is to include the addressee's name, the page number, and date near the top of the continuation pages. For example,

```
Carol Johnson              -2-            April 5, _____
```

Other forms are also acceptable as long as they look attractive and professional, and include sufficient information for easy reference. For example,

```
Carol Johnson                                     -2-
April 5, _____
```

> Johnson: April 4, _____   -2-

Leave one inch of blank space above and four single-spaced lines below, this reference information:

1"

4 lines

> Carol Johnson   -2-   April 4, _____
>
> and you should receive this information within the next three weeks. I would appreciate . . .

6. Closing

Your complimentary close can take various forms. The most standard and formal ones are

> Sincerely,
> Sincerely yours,
> Yours truly,
> Very truly yours,
> Cordially,
> Cordially yours,
> Faithfully,
> Faithfully yours,
> Respectfully,
> Respectfully yours,

On the other hand, it is acceptable to be a little more creative with your closings. If, for example, the purpose of your letter is to request information or action from the addressee, you might use one of these closings which re-emphasize the purpose of your letter:

Hopefully,
Waiting anxiously your reply,
Thanking you in advance,
Appreciatively,
Gratefully,
Requesting your assistance,

If you are withdrawing from consideration or turning down a job offer, you might end with some other type of creative closing:

Regretfully,
Apologetically,
Wishing my situation were different,
So sorry to pass on this,
Perhaps some other time,

Indeed, such nontraditional, creative closings may be more effective than the traditional formal closings. They make you and your letter stand out as different from the more routine and conformist business letter.

7. Signature Line

Your signature information should be on two lines. Your printed name should appear four spaces below the closing and your actual signature between the closing and printed name. If you don't reference your telephone number in the body of the letter, put it immediately after your name:

Sincerely,

Susan Thomas

Susan Thomas
Tel. 801/723-9851

Normally you should not over-formalize your signature information by assigning such titles to you as Mr., Mrs., Miss, and Ms. These titles tend to communicate greater social distance than you want to indicate to others. If, however, you have a professional title, such as "Dr.", you may want to include it with your signature information in order to emphasize your educational and professional background. In this case "Dr." should be specified with the proper initials after your name as either "Ph.D." or "M.D."

Susan Thomas, M.D.

Susan Thomas, Ph.D.

If you want to make your letter more personal, sign only your first name but type your full name. Use this personal approach only after you have established a relationship with someone by phone, letter, or in person—but not in your first encounter.

It's always more impressive to sign your name the old fashioned way— with a fountain pen rather than a ball point pen. Blue fountain pen ink contrasts nicely with black type and most paper colors. Fountain pen ink is still the sign of a professional and it adds a touch of class to the whole letter writing process. Use a fountain pen only if you can achieve a neat signature. A fountain pen signature is not a plus if it is smeared or awkward. Be sure your signature looks strong and confident.

8. Identification Initials

This is the first of four optional elements appearing in business letters. While these elements each serve an important function, their absence would not significantly alter the form, substance, or impact of your letters.

Identification initials are included when someone other than the sender transcribed/types the letter. The initials document who produced of the final letter. These initials take on various acceptable forms with the writer's initials always first, immediately followed by the initials of the transcriber/ typist:

TRS:AF   or   TRS/AF

trs:af   or   trs/af

TRSmith/af

Terrence R. Smith
AF

Normally, however, one does not have a secretary type a job search letter.

9. Enclosures

If you include some item or items with your letter, such as your résumé, make an "Enclosure" reference immediately after the identification initials. If more than one item is enclosed, specify the number after the word "Enclosure." This reference again documents who did what, and is important should the enclosures be missing, which sometimes happens. Proper forms include

> TRS:AF
> Enclosure
>
> TRS:AF
> Enclosures 2

10. Copy Reference

If a copy of your letter is also being sent to another party or parties, use a copy reference to indicate who is receiving the additional copies. The proper forms to use are these:

> TRS:AF
> cc: James Olson
>
> TRS:AF
> Enclosures 3
> cc: James Olson
> Mary Davis

11. Using Postscripts (P.S.)

Postscripts are used to include additional information in your letter. While it is acceptable to include postscripts, we only recommend using them under special circumstances. Postscripts tend to imply disorganized after-thoughts which distract the reader from your main message; they often convey lack of professionalism. Some writers use them improperly as dumping grounds for disconnected thoughts. On the other hand, some postscripts are useful to include, especially if your purpose is to re-emphasize or highlight an important point. This most often occurs in the case of sales letters where the writer's purpose is to make a final appeal or present a special last minute offer. In such a situation a postscript could give the letter added impact.

The postscript should begin two spaces following the identification initials, enclosure, or copy reference—whichever comes last. It might appear as:

P.S. John Davis asked me to send his regards.

P.S. I will be in your area Tuesday afternoon.

P.S. I will be out of town February 7-10.

Remember to use postscripts sparingly. Postscripts should only be used if they strengthen the impact of your message. If you forget to include certain information in the body of your letter, by all means retype the letter with the information included in the body rather than put it in a postscript as a disorganized after-thought.

Typing Styles

Several typing styles are acceptable for business letters. You have four major choices:

- Fully-blocked style
- Square-blocked style
- Modified-blocked style
- Semi-blocked style

Examples of each style, with corresponding elements keyed to each section, are found on pages 80 and 81.

The **fully-blocked style** begins all letter elements, except the heading on pre-printed letterhead, at the left-hand margin. Paragraphs are not indented.

The **square-blocked style** follows the same pattern with the exception that the date, initial and enclosure lines are placed near the right-hand margin. This form has two advantages: it gives the letter more of a balanced look and enables you to get more information on one page.

The **modified-blocked style** further rearranges the elements of the letter by placing the heading, date line, closing, and signature line near the right-hand margin. All other elements begin at the left-hand margin.

The **semi-blocked style** is similar to the modified-blocked style except the paragraphs are indented from five to ten spaces each. This form is one of the most widely used in business.

Layout and Design

Your letter should look clean, crisp, uncluttered, and professional. You can achieve such a look by paying particular attention to how it is laid out on a page. The cliche that "less is more" is a good rule to follow. Be generous with white space. Make sure the letter is centered top to bottom and left to right on the page. It's good to keep at least a 1¼" to 1½" margin around the page. A 1" margin begins to give letters a cluttered or unbalanced look.

> Keep your letter clean, crisp, and uncluttered. Be generous with white space. Use bullets and other visual elements for emphasis and readability.

You can emphasize important points in your letter, as well as improve its overall readability, by using various symbols such as bullets (●) or boxes (■). You can also emphasize by underlining, capitalizing, or changing type styles. However, be careful not to over-emphasize in this manner and thus create a very busy-looking letter. Many readers dislike having their reading flow broken frequently. You may want to emphasize by using only bullets and underlining, such as in the examples on pages 62 and 63.

Evaluation

Once you've completed a letter, examine the quality of its form, structure, and design according to the following evaluation criteria. Circle the numbers to the right that best describe the presence or absence of each element in your letter.

Elements	Yes	No
1. Makes an immediate good impression and is inviting to read.	1	3
2. First seven elements in letter (heading, date line, inside address, salutation, body, closing, signature lines) are present and adhere to the rules.	1	3

3.	Body of letter subdivided into 2 to 4 paragraphs.	1	3
4.	Most paragraphs average no more than 5 lines.	1	3
5.	Most sentences are 25 words or fewer in length.	1	3
6.	Includes complete name and address of letter recipient.	1	3
7.	Signed name strong and confidently.	1	3
8.	Selected a standard typing style.	1	3
9.	Has a clean, crisp, uncluttered, and professional look.	1	3
10.	Used a 1¼" to 1½" margin around the top, bottom and sides.	1	3

TOTAL [   ]

Add the numbers you circled to get a composite score. If your score comes to "10", your letter demonstrates strong elements of form, structure, and design. Correct any elements that receive a "3" so that your letter will become a perfect "10".

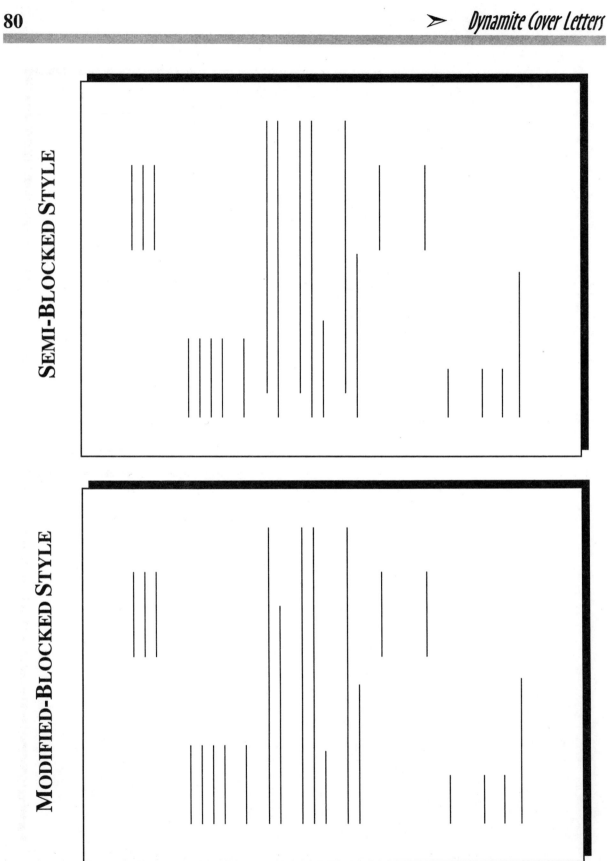

SEMI-BLOCKED STYLE

MODIFIED-BLOCKED STYLE

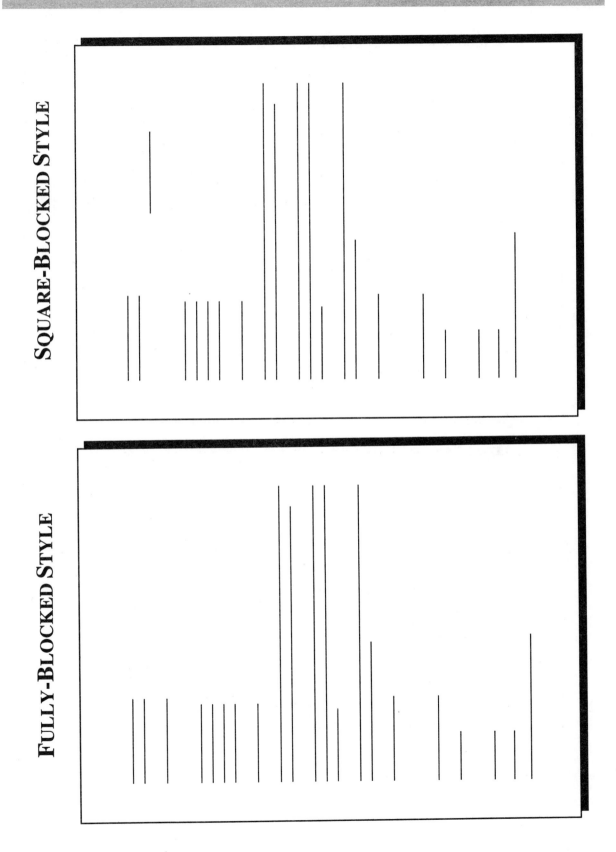

5

Organization and Content

A ssuming your letter is impressive enough to pass the five to ten second reading test, what you say and how you say it will largely determine if the reader will take desired actions. The power of your paper must move the reader to action. You can best do this by observing the rules of effective letter organization and content.

Common Mistakes

Individuals who receive hundreds of letters from job seekers report similar problems with most letters they read. These problems can be corrected by following a few simple organization and content rules. Letters that don't pass the five to ten second test tend to include several of these errors:

- **Looks unprofessional in form, structure, and design:** Many letters neglect the basic rules of form, structure, and design as outlined in Chapter 4. They look amateurish rather than reflect the professional competence of the writer. They don't demonstrate the writer's best professional effort.

- **Addressed to the wrong person or sent to the wrong place.** Many letter writers still forget to include proper contact information or send their letters to the wrong people and places. Make sure your letter includes a complete return address and a telephone number where you can be reached during the day. Also, closely check the name and address of the person who will receive your letter.

- **Does not relate to the reader's knowledge, interests, work, or needs.** Many letter writers fail to research the needs of their audience and target them accordingly. They simply waste employers' valuable time. If you respond to an ad or vacancy announcement, make sure you address the requirements specified for submitting your letter and résumé.

- **Includes spelling, grammatical, and punctuation errors.** The worst mistakes you can make in a letter are spelling, grammatical, or punctuation errors. These are unforgiving errors that clearly communicate your incompetence. Such mistakes demonstrate you are either careless or semi-illiterate—both deadly to a job search!

- **Uses awkward language and the passive voice.** Carefully watch your use of language and try to mainly use the active voice. The active voice gives your writing more energy. Good, crisp, interesting, and pleasing language is something few readers experience in reading letters.

- **Overly aggressive, assertive, boastful, hyped, and obnoxious in tone.** Employers receive many letters from individuals who try to impress them with what is essentially obnoxious language. They think that telling an employer they are the "hottest thing since sliced bread" will get them an interview. These letters even appear in some books that claim they are examples of "outstanding letters"! We have yet to encounter employers who are impressed by such letters. They tend to be low class letters that follow the principles of low class advertising.

- **Self-centered rather than job or employer-centered.** Too many job applicants still focus on what they want **from** employers (position, salary, benefits) rather than what they can do **for** employers (be productive, solve problems, contribute to organization, give benefits). Make sure your letters are oriented toward employers' needs. Tell them about the **benefits** you will give them. If you start referring to "you" rather than "I" in your letters, you will force yourself to be more employer-centered.

- **Poorly organized, difficult to follow, or wanders aimlessly.** Many letter writers still fail to plan the logic, sequence, and flow of their letters. They often begin with one idea, wander off to another idea, continue on to yet another disconnected idea, and then end the letter abruptly with no regard for transitions. Readers often must examine the letter two or three times to figure out what the writer wants. Such poor writing is inexcusable. If you can't say something in an organized and coherent manner, don't waste other peoples' time with your drivel!

- **Unclear what they are writing about or what they want.** Is there a goal or purpose to this letter? Many letters still lack a clear purpose or goal. They assume the reader will somehow figure out what they are writing about! Make sure your letter has a clear purpose. This should be revealed in the first paragraph.

- **Says little about the individual's interests, skills, accomplishments, or what they expect to achieve in the future.** Your job search letters should tell letter recipients what it is you can do for them. Unfortunately, many letter writers fail to communicate their strengths and benefits to potential employers.

- **Fails to include adequate contact information.** Be sure to include your complete address, including zip code, and a day-time telephone number. Do not use a P.O. Box number.

- **Dull, boring, and uninspired.** Employers are looking for individuals who have enthusiasm, energy, and fire. However, most letters they receive give little indication of these critical characteristics. Try to use language that expresses your enthusiasm, energy, and fire. At least start with the active voice!

- **Too long.** Busy people don't have time to read long letters. Chances are you can say just as much, and more effectively, in a short letter. Follow the principle of "less is best."

- **Poorly typed.** We still receive letters from people who use a typewriter with dirty keys and worn ribbons. They often make typing errors and then try to correct them with erasures, chalk tape, or correction fluids. Word processed letters often lack basic formatting, such as margins and centering; many are top heavy with the text occupying the first three inches of the page. The result is an amateurish looking letter that reflects poorly on the professional style and competence of the letter writer. If you write a job search letter, make sure it reflects your **best** professional effort.

- **Produced on cheap and unattractive paper.** Professional correspondence should be produced on good quality paper. However, many letter writers cut corners and go with poor quality paper. Don't be cheap. Good quality paper only costs a few cents more than the cheap product, and it's easy to find at your local stationery or print shop. It more than pays for itself.

- **Lacks information on appropriate follow-up actions**. In addition to indicating the writer's purpose, the letter should include information on what actions should or will be taken next. This information normally appears in the last paragraph.

In other words, many letters are just poorly written; they make poor impressions on readers. Letters that avoid these errors tend to be read and responded to. Make sure your letters are free of such errors!

Principles of Good Advertising

Several principles of effective advertising can be adapted to business writing and the job search. Indeed, the advertising analogy is most appropriate for a job search since both deal with how to best communicate benefits to potential buyers and users. These principles should assist you in developing your creative capacity to get what you want through letter writing.

Job search letters should be written according to the key principles of good advertising copy. They should include the following principles:

- **Catch the reader's attention:** While advertising copy primarily captures attention through a visual (headline, photo, illustration), a job search letter can do the same. It should project an overall quality appearance and an opening sentence or paragraph that immediately grabs the reader's attention. Like any good presentation, an attention-grabbing opening can be a question, startling statement, quotation, an example or illustration, humorous anecdote, a suspenseful observation, or a compliment to the reader. You must do this at the very beginning of your letter—not near the end which may never get read or where the reader's attention span has dissipated. You should always present your most important points first.

- **Persuade the reader about you, the product:** Good advertising copy involves the reader in the product by stressing **value and benefits**. It tells why the reader should acquire the product. A good job search letter should do the same—the product is you and the letter should stress the specific benefits the reader will receive for contacting you. The benefits you should offer are your skills and accomplishments as they relate to the reader's present and future needs. Therefore, you must know something about your reader's needs before you can offer the proper mix of benefits.

- **Convince the reader with more evidence:** Good advertising copy presents facts about the product that relate to its benefits. An effective job search letter should also present evidence of the writer's benefits. Statements of specific accomplishments and examples of productivity are the strongest such evidence.

- **Move the reader to take action (acquire the product):** Effective advertising copy concludes with a call to take action to acquire the product. This usually involves a convenient order form or a toll free telephone number. To stress the benefits of the product without moving the reader to take action would be a waste of time and money. When writing job search letters, you should conclude with a call to action. This is the ultimate power of paper. You want the reader to do something he or she ordinarily would not do—pick up the telephone to contact you, or write you a positive letter that leads to job search information, advice, and referrals as well as job interviews and offers. But we know few letters are so powerful as to move the reader to take initiative in contacting the letter writer. Simply put, the benefits are not as clear in a job search letter as they are in selling a product through advertising copy. Therefore, your call to action should mention that **you** will contact the reader by telephone at a certain time.

Form, style, content, production, and distribution all play important roles in communicating these persuasive elements in your letters.

Planning and Organizing

It goes without saying that you need to plan and organize your writing. By all means do not copy or edit a letter you think may be a good example of an effective job search letter. "Canned" letters tend to be too formal. Worst of all, they look and sound canned and thus they lack credibility.

Your letters should represent **you**—your personality, your credibility, your style, and your purpose. Start by asking yourself these questions **before** organizing and writing your letters:

- What is the **purpose** of this letter?

- What are the **needs** of my audience?

- What is a good opening sentence or paragraph for grabbing the **attention** of my audience?

- How can I maintain the **interest** of my audience?

- How can I best end the letter so that my audience will be **persuaded** to contact me?

- How much **time** should I spend revising and proofreading the letter?

- Will this letter represent my **best professional effort**?

After writing your letter, review these questions again. But this time convert them into a checklist for evaluating the potential effectiveness of your letter:

- Is the **purpose** of this letter clear?

- Does the letter clearly target the **needs** of my audience?

- Does the opening sentence or paragraph grab the **attention** of my audience?

- Does the letter state specific **benefits** for the reader?

- Does the letter sustain the **interest** of my audience?

- Will the letter **persuade** the reader to contact me?

- Have I spent enough **time** revising and proofreading the letter?

- Does the letter represent my **best professional effort**?

Always keep in mind what you want your audience to do in reference to your job search:

- Pay attention to your message.

- Remember you.

- Take specific actions you want taken.

Content Rules

The body of the letter should clearly communicate your message. How well you structure this section of the letter will largely determine how much impact it will have on your reader. You want to make sure the content of your letter speaks clearly to the needs of the reader.

The basic principles of effective communication are especially applicable to the body of your letter. In general you should:

1. **Have a clear purpose in writing your letter:** First ask yourself *"What message do I want to convey to my reader? What do I want him or her to do after reading my letter?"* Your message should be directly related to some desirable action or outcome.

2. **Plan and organize each section:** Each paragraph should be related to your overall purpose as well as to each other. The message should be logical and flow in sequential order. Start with a detailed outline of your message.

3. **Put your most important ideas first:** Since readers' attention decreases in direct relation to the length of a message, always state your most important points first.

4. **Keep your paragraphs short and your sentences simple:** Your reader is most likely a busy person who does not have time to read and interpret long and complex letters. The shorter the letter the better. Plain simple English is always preferred to complex usages which require the reader to re-read and decode your language. Three to four paragraphs, each three to five lines in length, should be sufficient. Keep sentences to no more than 25 words. Avoid including too many ideas in a single sentence.

5. **Your opening sentence should get the attention of the reader:** Your first sentence is the most important one. It should have a similar function as an advertisement—get the interest and involvement of your audience. Avoid the standard canned openers by making your sentence unique.

6. **Your opening paragraph should clearly communicate your purpose:** Get directly to the point in as short a space as possible. Remember, this is a business letter. Your reader wants to know why he should spend time reading your letter. Your first sentence should tell why and begin motivating him or her to take actions you desire.

7. **Your letter should convince the reader to take action:** Most letters function to inform and/or to persuade. In either case, they should lead to some action. Incorporate the four principles of good advertising in your letter writing:

- Catch the readers attention.
- Persuade the reader about you or your product—establish your credibility.
- Convince the reader with more evidence and benefits.
- Move the reader to acquire the service or product.

8. **Follow rules of good grammar, spelling, and punctuation:** Grammatical, spelling, and punctuation errors communicate a lack of competence and professionalism. Always check and re-check for such errors by (1) proofreading the letter yourself at least twice, and (2) asking someone else to proofread it also.

9. **Communicate your unique style:** Try to avoid standard or "canned" business language which is found in numerous how-to books on business writing and sample letters. Such language tends to be too formalistic and boring. Some examples go to the other extreme in presenting excessively aggressive and obnoxious letters which would turn off any normal employer. Write as if you were talking to a reader in a natural conversational tone. Be honest and straightforward in your message. Use your imagination in making your letter interesting. Put your personality into this letter. Try to demonstrate your **energy and enthusiasm** through your writing tone. For example, what type of impression does this letter leave on a reader?

> I'm writing in response to your recent ad for an assistant manager at your Great Falls Super store.
>
> Please find enclosed a copy of my résumé which outlines my experience in relationship to this position.
>
> Thank you for your consideration.

This is a typical cover letter received by many employers. While this letter is short and to the point, it doesn't grab the reader's attention, sustain his interest, nor move him to action. It screams "b-o-r-i-n-g!" It sounds like hundreds of canned cover letters employers receive each day. Why not try writing with more personality and energy? Consider this alternative:

Last year I increased profits by 15 percent at Star Drugs. It was a tremendous challenge, but the secret was simple—conduct the company's first management review which resulted in reorganizing the pharmaceutical and video sections. We eliminated two full-time employees and dramatically improved customer service.

I'm now interested in taking on a similar challenge with another company interested in improving its productivity. When I saw your ad in Sunday's <u>Toledo Star</u>, I thought we might share a mutual interest.

If you're interested in learning more about my experience, let's talk soon on how we might work together. I'll call you Thursday afternoon to answer any questions. In the meantime, please look over my enclosed résumé.

Which letter do you think will grab the attention of the employer and lead to some action? The first letter is both standard and boring. The second letter, equally true, incorporates most principles of effective letter writing—and advertising!

10. **Be personable by referring to "you" more than "I" or "we":** Your letters should communicate that you are other-centered rather than self-centered. You communicate your awareness and concern for the individual by frequently referring to "you."

11. **Try to be positive in what you say:** Avoid negative words and tones in your letters. Such words as "can't," "didn't," "shouldn't," and "won't" can be eliminated in favor of a more positive way of stating a negative. For example, instead of writing:

I don't have the required five years experience nor have I taken the certification test.

Try putting your message in a more positive tone by using positive content:

I have several years of experience and will be taking the certification test next month.

12. **Follow the basic ABC's of good writing:** These consist of <u>A</u>lways <u>B</u>eing:

- Clear
- Correct
- Complete
- Concise
- Courteous
- Considerate
- Creative
- Cheerful
- Careful

Inclusions and Omissions

What should be included and omitted in your cover letters? This question depends on your purpose and your audience. If you are responding to a vacancy announcement or a classified ad, you need to address the stated requirements for submitting an application. This usually involves a résumé and sometimes information on your "salary requirements."

Use the following general guidelines when trying to decide what to include or omit in your letters:

THINGS YOU SHOULD INCLUDE:

- Positive information that supports your candidacy.

- Information on your skills, abilities, strengths, accomplishments, interests, and goals.

- Examples of your productivity and performance.

- Benefits you can offer the reader.

- A daytime contact telephone number.

THINGS YOU SHOULD OMIT:

- Any extraneous information unrelated to the position, the employer's needs, or your skills.

- Any negative references to a former employer, your weaknesses, or the employer's organization and position.

- Boastful statements or proposed solutions to employer's problems.

- Salary requirements or history.

- References.

- Personal information such as height, weight, marital status, hobbies—information that also should not appear on a résumé.

One major question concerning many job applicants is whether or not to include salary information in their letter. Our general rule is to omit such information in letters; never volunteer salary information unless asked for it since this is the last question you want to deal with **after** you have demonstrated your value in job interviews. However, it is not always possible to avoid the salary question. In certain situations you must address this question in your letter. Job ads or vacancy announcements, for example, often request a statement about your salary requirements or salary history. If you don't respond, you may be eliminated from consideration. Be careful in how you respond to this requirement. When asked, state a **salary range** rather than a specific salary figure.

> Never volunteer salary information unless asked for it. Address the issue of salary within the context of the job interview—not in a letter.

If, for example, you currently make $40,000 a year but you expect to make $50,000 in your next job, you might state your salary expectation is *"in the range of $48,000 to $54,000."* When stating your salary history, make sure to include your total compensation package—not just your monthly salary figure.

The basic rule for including information in cover letters is to include only positive information that stresses your skills and abilities in reference to the employer's needs. Never, never, never volunteer your weaknesses or negatives. These are subjects which may be discussed during a job interview, but you should never put them in writing.

The biggest problem facing most job seekers is keeping focused on their goal. The job search is an intensely ego-involved activity that often goes astray due to a combination of wishful thinking and bouts of depression attendant with rejections. If you keep focused on your goals, what you include or omit in your cover letters will come naturally. You will know what should be communicated to employers as your qualifications.

Evaluation

Evaluate the quality of the organization and content of your letters by responding to the following evaluation criteria. Circle the numbers to the right that best describe your letter.

Characteristic	Yes	No
1. Immediately grabs the reader's attention.	1	3
2. Presents most important ideas first.	1	3
3. Expressed concisely.	1	3
4. Relates to the reader's interests and needs.	1	3
5. Persuades the reader to take action.	1	3
6. Free of spelling, grammatical, and punctuation errors.	1	3
7. Incorporates the active voice.	1	3
8. Avoids negative words and tones; uses positive language throughout.	1	3
9. Expresses the "unique you."	1	3
10. Employer-centered rather than self-centered.	1	3
11. Stresses benefits the reader is likely to receive from the letter writer.	1	3

12. Demonstrates a clear purpose.   1   3

13. Sentences and paragraphs flow logically.   1   3

14. Includes complete contact information
    (no P.O. Box numbers).   1   3

15. Expresses enthusiasm, energy, and fire.   1   3

16. Follows the ABC's of good writing.   1   3

                                        TOTAL

Add the circled numbers to arrive at your composite score. If you incorporate the principles identified in this chapter into the organization and content of your writing, your letter should score a perfect "16."

6

Top Quality Production

Whatever you do, make sure your letters look **and** feel professional. Remember, most employers review qualifications of strangers—people they don't know nor have learned to trust. Unfamiliar with the backgrounds and capabilities of most applicants, they work with limited information that provides only a few indicators of professional competence.

The production quality of your letters is an important indicator of your professional competence. You not only communicate your competence, style, judgment, and class through the form, structure, organization, and content of your letters (Chapter 4 and 5), you also communicate these same qualities at the production end. Therefore, you must create the right "look." This involves choosing the proper production equipment, type style and size, and paper quality and color. All such production factors must come together to produce dynamite letters for your successful job search.

Production Equipment

Your letters should always be neatly typed. While handwritten letters will give your job search a personal touch, this is not what you should be striving to achieve at this point in the job search. Handwritten letters are inappropriate when writing to employers. The general rule to follow is this: Employers want to see your best professional efforts. They are unforgiving of your errors. Poor judgment, improper style, and lack of class will be remembered as incompetence. Handwritten letters—including the more personalized thank-you letters —say nothing about your professional competence. They, instead, may say something about your judgment, or lack thereof!

What type of machine produces the most professional looking letters? Without a doubt a word processed letter produced on a laser printer looks best. Such machines produce error-free, letter quality products. They also demonstrate your best professional effort. However, if you don't have access to such equipment—which would surprise many employers who expect candidates to have at least this minimum level of technical expertise—at the very least you should produce your letters on a good quality typewriter. By "good quality" we mean one that gives a neat, clean appearance—no evidence of errors, such as strike-overs, erasures, or the use of correction fluids. However, keep in mind that you instantly communicate a low level of technical experience when you use a typewriter. Your choice of production equipment may communicate a negative message to an employer—you may need a great deal of training to *"get up to speed"* in today's workplace.

> **Employers want to see your best professional effort. They are unforgiving of errors. Make sure you produce perfect, error-free letters.**

This is not a good time to begin learning to type. If you can't type, or you consider yourself a poor typist who makes numerous mistakes, find someone to do this work for you. If need be, hire a professional word processor to produce your letters. It will be money well spent.

If your letters demonstrate your best professional effort, then there are no excuses for spelling or grammatical errors. Be sure you thoroughly proofread the final product. Better still, have someone else also proofread the letter as well as use the "spell-check" and "grammatik" functions on your word processing program.

Assuming you will use a word processor, make sure you print the letter on a letter quality printer. Many letter writers still use dot matrix printers that print fewer than 30 dots per character. They further compromise print quality by using worn ribbons—some haven't changed the original cloth ribbon since purchasing the printer! Such products look terrible even though they are produced on ostensibly higher level technology than a typewriter.

If your choices are between a non-letter quality dot matrix printer and a typewriter, go with the typewriter. Such dot matrix printers communicate the wrong message—your letter was probably mass produced similar to junk mail. Dot matrix printers should be used for drafting documents or printing data. They are best used for billing purposes—businesses report their accounts pay quicker when the bills are printed on dot matrix printers, because the assumption is the billing is computer-generated and thus more accurate than bills printed on letter quality machines. Job search letters produced on dot matrix printers communicate a lack of class as well as project a computer-generated, mass mailing image. However, many near letter quality dot matrix printers produce an acceptable look. When in doubt, hold the paper 15 inches from your nose and ask yourself this question: Does this letter look mass produced? If it does, change to a letter quality machine, or step down to a typewriter!

Perhaps the best test for evaluating the professional look of your letter is to find nine of the best looking business letters you have seen over the past year. Put your letter in the pile and then rank the ten according to their professional "look." If your letter doesn't look as good as the top three, start over and produce something more acceptable. Remember, your letter should demonstrate your best professional effort to employers.

Type Style and Size

The rule for selecting type style is this: go with something conventional that is also easy to read. If your word processing program and printer give type style choices, select one of the following: Courier, Bookface Academic, Prestige Elite, Times Roman, Palatino, New Century, or ITC Bookman. These are standard type styles appearing in most business letters, newspapers, magazines, and books. Avoid Helvetica, Gothic, Script, or any italicized style. While these are attractive styles for certain types of communication, they are more difficult to read compared to our first choices.

If your word processor permits you to vary type size, select a 10 to 12 point size, depending on the characteristics of the type style. Courier in 10 point, for example, is similar in size to Palatino in 11 point. You will probably want to stay close to 11 point. In some type styles 10 point is too small. In most type styles 12 point begins to look a bit large. For your reference, most of the text in this book is Times Roman style which is sized at 11.5 point.

Justification, Hyphens, Paragraphs

If you use a word processing program, consider making only the left side justified; leave the right side with an unjustified or ragged edge. Fully justified letters look too formal for some situations. Also, all words along the right-hand side should be complete words—no hyphens should break words. Make sure you double-space between paragraphs.

Paper Choices

The size, quality, and color of your paper also say something about your professional style and competence. You should be conventional once again. You should always type or print your letter on 8½" x 11" paper to fit into either a No. 10 business envelope or a 9" x 12" envelope. Smaller paper looks too personal and presents a weak image.

The paper you choose should both look and feel professional. Whatever you do, avoid copy machine, onion skin, or erasable papers. These look and feel cheap. For a few dollars you can purchase top quality paper at most stationery, office supply, or print shops. Choose 20 to 50 pound bond paper with a 100% cotton fiber or "rag content." If the paper has a definite texture to it, select one with a fine texture rather than one that looks and feels very coarse or rough. Avoid very thick papers as well as any scented papers.

Conventional paper colors for job search letters are white, off-white, ivory, or light grey. Contrary to what others may advise, basic white stationery is very acceptable today. It presents a clean, crisp look of class that may stand out next to the many off-white and ivory letters that flood today's job market. If you choose to go with light grey paper, keep it very light. Darker shades of any color can dull your message. Unless you are applying for an artistic or creative position, where you are expected to express a unique and unconventional style, avoid other colored papers.

It's best to send your letter in a matching envelope—same paper weight, texture, and color.

Produce a "10" Letter

Evaluate your final product in reference to the following checklist. Compare your letter according to each evaluation criteria and then rate it by circling the numbers to the right. When you finish, add the numbers circled for an overall cumulative score.

Characteristic	Yes	Maybe	No
1. Has an overall strong professional appearance sufficient to make an immediate favorable impression.	1	2	3
2. Used a new or nearly new ribbon with clean keys or printer head.	1	2	3
3. Adjusted copy setting properly—not too dark, not too light.	1	2	3
4. Type appears neat, clean, and straight.	1	2	3
5. Printed with a standard type style and size.	1	2	3
6. Produced on a letter quality machine.	1	2	3
7. Proofread and/or ran "spell-check" and "grammatik" for possible spelling and grammatical errors.	1	2	3
8. Used good quality paper stock that both looks and feels professional.	1	2	3
9. Selected a paper color appropriate for my audience.	1	2	3
10. Compared to nine other business letters received over the past year, this is one of the best in appearance.	1	2	3
TOTAL			

If your cumulative score is between 10 and 15, you are on the right track in producing professional looking letters. If your score is higher than 15, go back to the drawing broad. Keep improving the production quality of your letter until it receives a perfect "10"!

7

Effective Distribution

Distribution also plays an important role in demonstrating your best professional effort. How and to whom you send your letters does make a difference. Your method of delivery can elicit an immediate response or no response at all. While we do not recommend spending a great deal of time engaging in unconventional delivery methods—such as the story of the young man who sent his shoe in a shoebox accompanied by a "powerful" one sentence cover letter saying *"Now that I've got my shoe in the door, how about an interview?"*—you should at least pay attention to the details involved in effectively delivering your letters. While some unconventional methods work, many send the wrong messages about your mental state!

Distribution Choices and Etiquette

Your distribution choices are numerous. You may decide to shotgun (broadcast) a cover letter and résumé to hundreds of "Dear Sir/Madam" employers or selectively target only ten employers by their correct name and title. You may decide to raise the attention and response level of your letter recipients by using special next-day delivery services or enclose your letter in a brightly printed, attention-getting envelope. Or you may decide to type the letter but handwrite the address as well as affix a nice commemorative stamp to the envelope.

Another set of important distribution issues concerns the medium for sending your message. What's the proper etiquette? Should you primarily confine your distribution activities to using the mail or is it okay to fax and e-mail your correspondence? The rule here is very simple: only fax or e-mail correspondence if asked to do so by the employer. Unsolicited faxes and e-mail may anger employers who often reserve these communication channels for private correspondence—to be used *"by invitation only."* Most employers consider physical mail delivery systems (USPS, Federal Express, UPS, RPS, Avery, DHL, Airbourne, etc.) to be the proper channels through which strangers should send their correspondence.

While these considerations may initially appear insignificant, or even petty, in comparison to your seemingly more important letter and résumé messages, they can and do make a difference in how quickly and how well your letters are read and responded to. Remember, you are essentially a stranger in the eyes of most employers. Neglect these distribution issues and you may seriously impair your job search.

The Envelope

> Use a 9" x 12" envelope to mail your letter and résumé. This size envelope presents your materials nicely and stands out from the crowd.

In most cases you should send your letter in a matching No. 10 business envelope. However, if your letter is accompanied by a résumé or other printed materials, you may want to use a 9" x 12" envelope. This large envelope presents your materials better to the recipient. It stands out from other envelopes. More importantly, it means your materials will arrive neat and flat. The receiver need not unfold your letter or struggle to keep it flat should the paper tend to spring back to the folded position.

Try to select an envelope that matches the color, weight, and texture of your letter. However, if you choose a 9" x 12" envelope, you may not be able to match it with the stationery. In this case either use a plain white or manila (tan) envelope or select an attention-getting color—red, orange, or blue will stand out. Alternatively, you may choose a special pre-printed priority or next-day envelope available at the Post Office or through UPS, Federal Express, or a courier service. All of these envelopes stand out from the crowd of No. 10 business envelopes.

We recommend typing the address on the envelope. Some people claim a handwritten address is more personal and thus more powerful. However, it's not as professional as a neatly typed address. Be sure to include your return address in the upper left-hand corner. You should never affix a pressure sensitive mailing label to a No. 10 business envelope. Such labels look like machine affixed addresses and thus immediately downgrade letters to junk mail.

How will you affix the postage? Many people claim it's better to personalize the postage by using a nice commemorative stamp. Others say it's best to affix the postage by postal meter since it looks more professional since this is the standard way businesses affix their postage. This is probably another one of those proverbial *"six one way, half a dozen another"* type of decisions. In the end, it may not make much difference. When in doubt, use postage stamps. A postage meter may give the wrong impression—you are "stealing" postage from your present employer.

Should you decide to broadcast hundreds of letters and résumés to those "Dear Sir/Madam" employers, it really doesn't make much difference how you affix the postage. In fact, since you already decided to make your letter impersonal, and you probably won't get many positive responses, you might as well save some money and send them the least expensive way possible.

To Whom It May Concern

It's always preferable to address your letter to a specific person by name. If you don't, chances are your letter will be thrown away or given little attention. After all, why should someone take you and your job search seriously if you won't take them seriously enough to at least learn their name? If you don't know to whom you should send your letter, you should make a few phone calls to find out. Call the organization and ask the operator or receptionist some version of this question:

> Hi, I need some information. I'm sending a letter to the head of the marketing department, but I'm not sure I have the correct name and address. Could you help me?

This question will easily get you the correct information from someone who will quickly volunteer the correct information. You also might want to ask for the person's phone number. After all, you'll later need this number for follow-up purposes. It only takes a phone call and a few seconds of your time to get this information. Don't be *"pennywise but pound foolish"* or lazy in literally addressing your letter to no one!

If you decide to broadcast your résumé to hundreds of organizations, you obviously have decided to use a junk mail approach to employers. In this case, you probably will not address your letters to a specific name unless you have access to a specialized mailing list that includes the names appropriate to your job search. If you lack names, at least address your letters to a position, such as "Director of Personnel," "Director of Marketing," "Vice-President of Manufacturing," or "Director of Public Affairs." Assuming the mail room does not discard it, your letter should find its way to the proper person. As we noted in a previous chapter, avoid sexist, anonymous, and wimpish salutations such as "Dear Sir," "To Whom It May Concern," or "Gentlepeople." If you know the position, open your letter with the name of the position: "Dear Director" or "Dear Vice-President." You may want to eliminate the salutation altogether. However, don't hold your breath in expectation of receiving an avalanche of responses from such generic letters!

> Address your correspondence to a specific person by name. If you don't have a name, call to get this information. Without a name, you're essentially sending junk mail.

Best Methods

What's the best way to send your letters? Most job search letters are sent first-class through the regular mail. However, if you really want to make an impression on an employer and seek an immediate response, send it by special overnight or next-day air services. These services are conveniently available through the U.S. Postal Service, Federal Express, UPS, or other couriers. Such services may cost anywhere from $9.00 to $35. While your mail will probably be signed for in the mail room or by a receptionist, it should be handled separately and delivered quickly to the individual.

While these services may get the recipient's immediate attention, they do not guarantee immediate action nor positive responses. What they do is shorten the time span between when you send the letter and when you speak with the recipient about the letter. You will still need to follow-up with a telephone call. Make sure you call the same day the individual is supposed to receive your letter. Since most of these special services guarantee delivery by 11am, make your telephone call sometime between 2pm and 4pm that same day. When you do call, mention that you sent your letter by special overnight delivery service. The delivery service itself becomes the lead in for your telephone conversation. Introduce yourself by asking if the individual received your letter that morning. You might say something like this:

> Hi, this is Mary Stafford. I'm calling in reference to a letter I sent you yesterday by Federal Express. Did you receive it this morning? Have you had a chance to read it yet?

The individual will most likely remember receiving your letter. If not, chances are he or she will look for it immediately to verify receiving it. With this phone call, you increase the likelihood your letter will get read and responded to. By sending it for next day delivery, your letter recipient should be better prepared to discuss your letter—and remember you.

You also can register or certify your letter to get the attention of your letter recipient. However, this service delivers your letter in two to three days, or perhaps longer. If you want to make an impression and get immediate feedback, go with the special overnight delivery services which guarantee a morning delivery.

Never fax your letter or résumé unless requested to do so by someone. The poor quality of fax paper and images will not enhance your professional image. If someone requests you to fax your letter and/or résumé, make sure you also put your original copies in the mail. Type at the top left side of the letter the date you faxed the information: "Faxed July 9." Also, immediately follow-up your fax with a phone call to make sure the fax was received; ask if the individual has any questions or needs any additional information.

Targeting

The most effective letters are targeted on specific individuals. They demonstrate some knowledge of the individual and his organization. This knowledge is gained through research on the organization or acquired through referrals received as part of your networking activities. If you demonstrate your knowledge of the individual and the organization, or initiate the letter through a referral and follow-up with a phone call, your letter recipient should be responsive to you. If you make a habit of writing three targeted letters each day, you will begin building a large network of employer contacts that will eventually turn into job interviews and offers. However, you must be doggedly persistent in writing targeted letters and following-up with phone calls.

Broadcasting and Junk Mail

If you choose to broadcast letters and résumés to hundreds of potential employers, be perfectly honest with yourself. This is not the most productive use of your job search time nor money. You're engaging in a junk mail exercise that will be lucky to elicit more than a one percent positive response rate. Many first-time junk mail users have unrealistic expectations of the effectiveness of such strategies. Many questionable employment firms that promote résumé and letter writing services tied to customized mailing lists and printing services promote such unrealistic expectations; some charge over $2,000 and produce near scandalous results! Unfortunately, many job seekers still engage in wishful thinking when they resort to this direct mail activity. They are reaching hundreds of employers they would not otherwise reach through targeted letters and telephone calls. They believe their phone will start ringing any day with many invitations to interview.

> **Broadcasting letters and résumés to hundreds of employers is an exercise in wishful thinking. Don't expect more than a 1% response rate.**

The hard realities of job search junk mail are often these: no responses and a few *"Thank you, we'll keep your résumé on file"* or *"Sorry, we have no positions at present for someone with your qualifications"* letters. These responses should not be taken as hopeful signs of an impending job vacancy for which you will be considered. They are merely polite rejections penned by employers who are unwilling to give job applicants all of the bad news—they have thrown your résumé and letter away!

Following-Up With Impact

Writing letters without following-up is a recipe for communication failure. Always think of the processes of writing, producing, and distributing as the first three steps in a four-step letter effectiveness process. Following-up is the critical fourth step which determines whether or not your letter is read and responded to. If you fail to follow-up, you kill your chances of experiencing the fruits of the first three steps.

Always keep in mind that few busy people immediately respond to letters with a letter, phone call, fax, or e-mail. You should never assume someone is neither interested in you nor are they inconsiderate for not responding to your letter. Why should they respond just because you decide to take their time intruding into their daily work routines by writing a letter? If they responded to every letter they receive each day, they would not have time to get any of their work done! Instead, approach this situation from a different assumption altogether. When you send your letter, assume your recipient is a very busy person who will not respond unless you complete the fourth step in the letter effectiveness process. Their response is contingent upon the quality of your follow-up activities. In fact, a typical recipient of a job search letter will quickly read it and then put it aside so they can get back to their more important daily work.

> **If you want a response to your letter, you must take the initiative to follow-up with a phone call.**

Therefore, if you want a response to your letter, **you** must take the initiative to follow-up with a phone call. Your call will generate a response. In some cases, the individual may not remember receiving your letter and thus requests you to send another copy by mail or fax. Your follow-up activities will quickly educate you on the difficulties inherent in managing job search communications. You will learn most people who receive your letters are very busy people who have difficulty remembering any one letter or résumé received on a particular day or week. Busy people have deadlines, priorities, meetings to attend, and decisions to make. Seriously reading unsolicited mail is a luxury few busy people can afford. Regardless of how intrinsically good your letter may be, it still must compete with many other letters each day. In the end, what may make your letter stand out and be remembered amidst the crowd are your follow-up activities. We will examine these activities in the next chapter.

Evaluating

Examine the potential effectiveness of your letter distribution activities by responding to the following evaluation criteria:

Action	Yes	No
1. Addressed to a specific name.	1	3
2. Used a No. 10 business or a 9" x 12" envelope.	1	3
3. Checked to make sure all enclosures got enclosed.	1	3
4. Matched the envelope paper stock and color to the stationery (if No. 10 business envelope).	1	3
5. Typed the address and return address.	1	3
6. Affixed a commemorative stamp.	1	3
7. Used a special delivery service for overnight delivery.	1	3
8. Followed-up letter immediately with a phone call.	1	3
TOTAL		

If you answer "no" to any item other than No. 7 or your cumulative score is higher than 8, be sure to make the necessary changes. This is not the time and place to make mistakes that can negatively affect the overall quality of your letter and accompanying materials.

8

Dynamite Implementation and Follow-Up Techniques

We've always been fascinated why people read "how-to" job search books but never seem to get their job search on track. Many people find such books "interesting" and "helpful." They may even attend a job search seminar or take a college course on the subject. Some even become book and seminar "junkies"; they repeat the process of reading more job search books and attending more seminars. Some get stuck trying to do a self-assessment, continuously asking themselves *"Who am I?"* and *"Where am I going in life?"* They seem preoccupied with contemplating their future rather than interested in contacting, meeting, and getting feedback from potential employers. Others crank out résumés and cover letters which they send to only five employers. They wait and they wait and they wait. Then they wonder why there seem to be so few jobs available and why no one wants to hire them.

From Advice to Action

So they read another book and discover they did everything that they were told to do, but nothing seems to happen to them. Maybe the book was bad, or maybe they aren't good. Somehow all this "how-to" advice doesn't seem to work. In the meantime, they engage in a great deal of wishful thinking that somehow the ideal job will come their way if only they read more books and attend more seminars!

Let's be honest with ourselves and all the "how-to" advice you encounter. Good jobs do not come by way of understanding a process nor by way of osmosis. They only come your way if you take the necessary **actions** to bring them within the scope of your job search. You must take certain actions and repeat them over and over again. Those actions must go beyond reading more books and attending more job search seminars. It's time to free yourself of the books and get on with the business of making things happen on a daily basis.

Implementation For Results

The basic failure with most job searches is the inability to implement and follow-through. Individuals may learn all the tricks to writing effective letters and résumés as well as how to conduct effective interviews and negotiate salaries. But if they don't translate their **understanding** into concrete and purposeful **repetitive actions**, they will go nowhere with their job search.

> The basic failure with most job searches is the inability to implement and follow-through. You must translate your understanding into concrete and repetitive actions.

The process of translating understanding into action is what we call **implementation**—the ability to make things happen according to plan. At the very heart of implementation is the repetitive process of **follow-up**. Without an effective follow-up campaign focused on all of your job search communications and actions, your job search is likely to flounder. You'll become a resident of that never-never land of "no responses" to your letters.

Commit Yourself in Writing

At the very least, implementation requires you to put together an action plan and commit yourself to seeing it become a reality. You may find it useful to commit yourself in writing to implementing your job search. This is a very useful way to get both motivated and directed for action. Start by completing the job search contract on page 111 and keep it near you—in your briefcase or

JOB SEARCH CONTRACT

1. I will begin my job search on _____.
   (specific date)

2. I will involve _____ with my job search.
   (individuals/groups)

3. I will complete my skills identification step by _____.
   (specific date)

4. I will complete my objective statement by _____.

5. I will complete my résumé by _____.

6. I will complete my first round of job search letters (approach and cover) by _____.

7. I will begin my networking activities on _____.

8. Each week I will:

   - make ___ new job contacts.
   - write ___ job search letters.
   - conduct ___ informational interviews.
   - follow-up on ___ referrals.

9. I expect my first job interview will take place during the week of _____.

10. I expect to begin my new job by _____.

11. I will manage my time so that I can successfully complete my job search and find a high quality job.

Signature: _____

Date: _____

on your desk.

In addition, you should complete weekly performance reports. These reports identify what you actually accomplished rather than what your good intentions tell you to do. Make copies of the performance and planning report form on page 113 and use one each week to track your actual progress and to plan your activities for the next week.

If you fail to meet these written commitments, issue yourself a revised and updated contract. But if you do this three or more times, we strongly suggest you stop kidding yourself about your motivation and commitment to find a job. Start over again, but this time consult a professional career counselor who can provide you with the necessary structure to make progress in finding a job.

A professional may not be cheap, but if paying for help gets you on the right track and results in the job you want, it's money well spent. Don't be "penny wise but pound foolish" with your future.

The Art of Follow-Up

Follow-up is a much neglected art, but it is the key to unlocking employers' doors and for achieving job search success. But many people fear following-up. Like giving a speech, it requires talking with strangers! In fact, they would rather put their letters in the mail and wait for the telephone to ring or for a return letter.

Follow-up occurs at the implementation stage of your job search. It is the single most important element for converting communications into action. Without an effective follow-up campaign, your letters and résumés are likely to lose their impact. They will probably sit on someone's desk amidst numerous other letters and résumés. If you want dynamite job search letters—ones that move readers to actions that eventually lead to job interviews and offers—you must engage in a series of follow-up activities that will give your letters their intended impact.

How to Kill a Perfect Letter

It only takes seven simple words to kill a job search letter and thereby deaden your job search:

I look forward to hearing from you.

WEEKLY JOB SEARCH PERFORMANCE AND PLANNING REPORT

1. The week of: _____.

2. This week I:

   ▪ wrote ____ job search letters.
   ▪ sent ____ résumés and ____ letters to potential employers.
   ▪ completed ____ applications.
   ▪ made ____ job search telephone calls.
   ▪ completed ____ hours of job research.
   ▪ set up ____ appointments for informational interviews.
   ▪ conducted ____ informational interviews.
   ▪ received ____ invitations to a job interview.
   ▪ followed-up on ____ contacts and ____ referrals.

3. Next week I will:

   ▪ write ____ job search letters.
   ▪ send ____ résumés and ____ letters to potential employers.
   ▪ complete ____ applications.
   ▪ make ____ job search telephone calls.
   ▪ complete ____ hours of job research.
   ▪ set up ____ appointments for informational interviews.
   ▪ conduct ____ informational interviews.
   ▪ follow-up on ____ contacts and ____ referrals.

4. Summary of progress this week in reference to my Job Search Contract commitments:

   _____

   _____

   _____

   _____

Even five words will do it: *"Thank you for your consideration."* If you close your letters with these standard statements, you effectively kiss your letter and résumé goodbye! You'll be lucky if five percent of your letter recipients will take the initiative to contact you based on these closing statements.

Such statements are the most commonly used closings in job search letters. They are also the most ineffective closings. Consider for a moment what the seven word statement means. What are you saying? Do you want the letter recipient to give you a call? If this is what you mean—and a literal reading of this sentence confirms such an expectation—then you are in for a big disappointment.

Why should a busy person bother writing you—a stranger who is trying to get something out of them—a letter or giving you a telephone call? Just because you expect it or because it's a nice thing to do? Let's get our heads turned on straight and deal with the realities of business communication etiquette. No one owes you a letter or telephone call just because you decided to interrupt their schedule with a job search letter. This statement basically says you really don't care if you ever hear from the reader. Accordingly, you will most likely not hear from the reader. Not that the reader is inconsiderate or not interested in talking with you. It's just that your letter initiative provided no follow-through mechanisms for making the connection other than expecting the reader to call you! It is simply inconsiderate on your part to expect the person to contact you. What should they contact you about? Acknowledge receiving your letter? Share their experience with you? Give you some job leads? Offer you a job? Wish you well? What exactly is it you want the reader to contact you about?

> **No one owes you a letter or telephone call just because you decided to interrupt their schedule with a letter.**

Rescuing Your Letter

It's incumbent upon **you** to take follow-up initiative. The first thing you need to do is to never, never, never end your letter with those six or seven deadly words. Instead, always complete your letter with a **follow-up statement** which calls for **you** to initiate a specific **action** related to the contents of your letter. These statements can come in many different forms:

➤ I will call your office Tuesday afternoon, July 17, to see if your schedule would permit us to meet briefly.

➤ I know you're very busy. But I also know I could benefit greatly from your advice. Could I call you on Wednesday morning to briefly discuss my interests? I'll only take a few minutes of your time.

➤ I will call your office at 2:30pm on Thursday, July 19, to ask you a few questions about my interests and to see if we might be able to get together for a brief meeting in the near future.

➤ Would next week be a good time to discuss my interests? I'll call your office at 3pm on Monday, July 16, to check your schedule. I appreciate your time.

Notice that each statement specifies **what** you will do and **when** you will do it —an expected action. The reader now knows what to expect next from you. At this stage he or she needs to do nothing other than **remember** you and your letter—the most important outcome you want to achieve when initially developing a communication link with your reader.

Being remembered is extremely important to an effective job search. Individuals who get remembered are those whose letters get read and who receive referrals. Put yourself in the shoes of the reader. Assume you receive 25 job search letters a day. Twenty-two writers end their letters with the seven deadly words. Three writers close by saying they will call the reader at a specific time to discuss the questions, issues, or interests raised in the letter. Which of the 25 letters are you most likely to remember, especially when you have a calendar facing you on your desk telling you the phone is likely to ring at particular times during the next few days? You will probably re-read the letters from the three individuals who said they would call. You want to determine if it's worth taking the calls. In addition, you want to prepare for each call by acknowledging receipt of the letter and demonstrating your knowledge of its contents. You may also want to ask a few questions. If on re-reading the letter you decide you really don't want to talk to this individual, then you will be prepared to nicely say "no" when you take the call or you will give this message to one of your staff members who will nicely tell the caller that you really don't have time, you can't help them, and you wish them "good luck".

In either case, as the letter writer your follow-up actions lead to desirable outcomes. If you are able to talk directly with the individual, you will most likely acquire useful information. If you get a rejection, you at least know you need not waste anymore time with this potential contact. Go on to other more promising job search connections.

Effective Follow-Up Options

You have basically two follow-up options. You can write another letter requesting a response to your first letter or you can telephone the person. Writing another letter merely attempts to force the reader to take the initiative in contacting you—not our idea of a bright follow-up activity. You're merely moving more paper onto the individual's already crowded desk. Your first follow-up letter will most likely not generate the intended response. However, your fourth or fifth follow-up letter will probably be acknowledged. At this point you have sufficiently pestered the person into action. Pestered people tend to respond in two different ways:

- They feel guilty for not having responded to you earlier and thus are very willing to discharge this professional obligation by spending some time talking with you and giving you useful information.

- They feel put upon by strangers who have no business expecting them to take valuable time to respond to the writer's "personal" matters. They write a short letter acknowledging your communications and telling you they can't help or aren't interested in further contacts with you.

However, pestering people and putting them on guilt trips is no way to conduct an effective job search.

Your second follow-up option is a telephone call. This is our preferred follow-up method. It's both efficient and effective. But keep in mind two important characteristics of a follow-up telephone call that can have a positive or negative affect on your job search:

- **It is probably your first verbal contact with the individual** after having communicated via the written word and paper. As such, this call may become your first **interview** even though you are only attempting to ask a few questions or set up an appointment. Be prepared to conduct an interview as soon as you make this follow-up call. The individual may not want to see you, but would be happy to answer any questions you have over the telephone. This means being prepared with specific questions, knowing how to answer questions, and projecting yourself properly over the telephone. You should have a pleasing telephone voice and sound coherent (complete sentences, no repetitious "uhs" or "ya know" or high-pitched voices). Keep in mind what's happening in this telephone encounter: your letter recipient is now associating a voice with your written materials. What you say and how you say it may determine if the individual wants to also see your face by scheduling a face-to-face interview!

- **Telephone follow-ups can be very frustrating.** You will be lucky to directly contact the person on your first, second, or even third phone call. The person may be out of the office, attending an important meeting, or avoiding you altogether. In some cases it may take eight phone calls before you can speak directly with the person! In other cases you may never get to talk to the person—only receive a message through a gatekeeper.

Multiple Follow-Ups

Conducting an effective follow-up is easier said than done. A typical follow-up may require three to seven phone calls because the person is unavailable or avoiding your call. With each phone call you may need to leave a message. However, similar to response rates to letters, don't expect busy people to return phone calls from strangers. Many people only do so after the third or fourth redundant phone message—guilt moves them to action!

Whatever you do, please do not show your irritation, anger, or disappointment in not having your phone calls returned. Some people feel insulted and express the irritation in their tone of voice or choice of words when they make their third, fourth, or fifth ineffective follow-up call:

➤ Well, I left two messages—one on Tuesday and another on Wednesday.

➤ Does he usually return his phone calls?

➤ What should I do? I keep calling but he won't return my calls!

➤ Did he leave a message for me?

➤ How many more days should I wait before I call again?

These responses communicate the wrong attitude toward someone who may be able to assist you. While they may accurately reflect what's happening, they lack tack and good job search manners. Keep your cool and cheerfully keep leaving messages as if you understand this is what normally happens in the course of conducting follow-up calls.

A standard follow-up scenario goes something like this. You stated in your letter you would call at 2:30pm on Tuesday. When you call you will probably have to go through one or two gatekeepers before you can make direct contact with the person you want to reach. The final gatekeeper will probably be a personal secretary or receptionist who is well versed on the art of screening important from not-so-important calls. When the final gatekeeper takes your call, the following exchange is likely to occur:

SECRETARY: Mr. Carroll's office. How can I help you?

YOU: Hi, this is Mary Harris calling for Mr. Carroll.

SECRETARY: I'm sorry, Mr. Carroll is not available.

YOU: When would you expect him to be free?

SECRETARY: I don't know. He's been in meetings all day. Could I take a message and have him return your call?

YOU: Yes, would you please? My name is Mary Harris and my telephone number is _____. I'm calling in reference to a letter I sent Mr. Carroll on July 5. I mentioned I would be calling him today.

SECRETARY: I'll give him the message.

YOU: Thanks so much for your help.

Don't hold your breath in expectation of getting a return call soon. The secretary will give him the message, but he probably will sit on it and do nothing until he's motivated to do so. Consequently, you will probably need to initiate another call. If you don't hear from the person within 24 hours, make another follow-up call. This time your conversation may go something like this:

SECRETARY:	Mr. Carroll's office. How can I help you?
YOU:	Hi, this is Mary Harris calling for Mr. Carroll.
SECRETARY:	I'm sorry, Mr. Carroll is not available. Can I take a message?
YOU:	Yes. Can you tell him Mary Harris called. My telephone number is _____. I'm calling in reference to my letter of July 5. I also called yesterday and left a message.
SECRETARY:	Oh, yes. I remember your call. I did give him the message. However, he's been extremely busy. I'll make sure he gets the message again.

You may get a return call, but don't hold your breath. You will probably need to initiate another call or two before you make direct contact. Again, wait 24 hours to call again. With a third call you will most likely have the attention of both the secretary and the letter recipient. Both may start to feel somewhat guilty for not taking your call. The secretary especially feels responsible because she obviously has been ineffective vis-a-vis both you and her boss. The letter recipient is beginning to collect a pile of messages indicating the same person is waiting for a return call. At this point the secretary is likely to make certain decisions: the next time you call she will make a special effort to remind her boss that you have called several times, and it would be nice to return the call or give a more hopeful response than "I'll give him the message"; or she will ask her boss if she should relay any special message to Mary Harris should she call again. Your fourth follow-up call will usually result in a change in dialogue with the secretary:

SECRETARY:	Mr. Carroll's office. How can I help you?
YOU:	Hi, this is Mary Harris calling for Mr. Carroll.
SECRETARY:	Yes, I remember you called earlier. I'm sorry he hasn't been able to get back with you. He's been so busy these past few days. When I spoke with him yesterday, he said he'd call you today around 4pm.

Making several follow-up phone calls demonstrates persistence. While it's unfortunate you must make so many follow-up calls, especially if they are expensive long-distance calls, that's the reality of communicating in today's business world. Such persistence pays off because you become remembered and because individuals feel guilty about not returning your calls after receiving the same message over and over from the same person.

Follow-Up Your Follow-Up

Once you make telephone contact, be sure to follow-up this follow-up call with a nice thank-you letter. Again, your goal is not just to get useful job information. Your goal should also include being **remembered** for future reference. You want busy people to remember you because they are likely to refer you to other busy people who may be looking for individuals with your qualifications. In other words, the thank-you follow-up letter becomes an important building block for expanding your network for information, advice, and referrals. Job seekers who follow-up their follow-up calls with a thank-you letter are more likely to be remembered that those who merely hang up the phone and move on to other follow-up calls.

Follow-Up Really Means Following-Up

It's funny what you learn about people through their letters. Today more and more job seekers close their letters with an effective follow-up statement, but they never follow-up. They simply don't do what they say they will! Indeed, the last three letters we received from job seekers included the date and time they would call us to follow-up. They wrote nice letters—modeled after the advice of "how-to" job search letter books—but we have yet to hear from them. Somewhere along the way to the mailbox no one told them they actually had to follow-up their letter! Yes, we remember these people, but unfortunately we remember them for what they did to us—wasted our time with a canned follow-up statement they had no intentions of doing anything about.

You simply can't do more damage to your job search than failing to follow-up according to expectations. Many people say they will call on Thursday afternoon, but they never call. It's as if the action follow-up statement has become a routine and meaningless closing for job search letters. Many job seekers merely go through the motions of putting in a "canned" closing statement. Indeed, one wonders how much else in the letter is "canned" or "creatively plagiarized" from examples of "outstanding" cover letters.

Whatever you do, make sure your letters represent **you**. Moreover, make sure you **do** exactly what you say you will do. If you tell your reader you will call them at 2:30 on Thursday afternoon, make sure you call exactly at that time. The person may have penciled-in this time on their calendar to speak with you. If you fail to do so, the individual is likely to remember you in negative terms—this job seeker doesn't follow-through or make appointments! You simply can't recover from such an initial negative impression. You will be wasting both your time and the time of the reader.

Evaluate Your Follow-Up Competencies

Let's evaluate the potential effectiveness of your follow-up activities. Respond to each of the following statements by indicating how you dealt with each follow-up action:

Follow-Up Actions	Yes	No
1. Completed the "Job Search Contract."	1	3
2. Completed my first "Weekly Job Search Performance and Planning Report."	1	3
3. Ended my letter with an action statement indicating I would contact the individual by phone within the next week.	1	3
4. Made the first follow-up call at the time and date indicated in my letter.	1	3
5. Followed-up with additional phone calls until I was able to speak directly with the person or received the requested information.	1	3
6. Maintained a positive and professional attitude during each follow-up activity. Was pleasantly persistent and tactful during all follow-up calls. Never indicated I was irritated, insulted, or disappointed in not having my phone calls returned.	1	3

7. Followed-up the follow-up by sending a thank-
   you letter genuinely expressing my appreciation
   for the person's time and information.   1   3

                                    TOTAL

Add the numbers you circled to the right of each statement to get a cumulative
score. If your score is higher than "7", you need to work on improving your
follow-up competence. Go back and institute the necessary changes in your
follow-up behavior so your next letter will be a perfect "7"!

9

Evaluate Your Effectiveness

Evaluation should play a central role in all of your job search activities. If you want to be most effective, you must continuously evaluate your progress throughout each step of your job search. Evaluation based upon specific performance criteria eliminates a great deal of wishful thinking that can confuse and misdirect your job search. Best of all, evaluation helps keep your job search **focused on goals and productive activities** that eventually lead to job interviews and offers.

Conduct Two Evaluations

Be sure to conduct two types of evaluations related to your letters. The first is an **internal evaluation**. This is a self-evaluation you conduct by examining your actions in reference to specific performance criteria. Questionnaires appear at the end of Chapters 4, 5, 6, 7, and 8 for evaluating how to best structure, organize, produce, distribute, and follow-up your letters.

The second type of evaluation may be more important than the internal evaluation. This is an **external evaluation** which is conducted by someone other than yourself. You ask individuals whose judgment you respect to give you feedback on your job search actions. In the case of letters, you want to find two or three individuals who will read your letters and then give you frank feedback on your writing strengths and weaknesses. This external evaluation is the closest you will get to receiving realistic feedback from the actual letter recipient.

Internal Evaluation

Once you complete your first job search letter, conduct a thorough internal evaluation based upon the following criteria. Several of these criteria already appeared in previous chapters. They relate to each step in the letter writing process—structure, organization, production, distribution, and follow-up activities. Respond to each statement by circling the appropriate number to the right that most accurately describes your letter.

	AUDIENCE	**Yes**	**Maybe**	**No**
1.	I know the needs of my audience based upon my research of both the organization and the individual.	1	2	3
2.	My letter clearly reflects an understanding of the needs of the organization and the letter recipient.	1	2	3
3.	The letter recipient will remember me favorably based on the unique style and content of my letter.	1	2	3
4.	My letter speaks the language of the employer—goals and benefits.	1	2	3
	FORM, STRUCTURE, AND DESIGN			
5.	Makes an immediate good impression and is inviting to read.	1	2	3
6.	First seven elements in letter (heading, date line, inside address, salutation, body, closing, signature lines) are present and adhere to the rules.	1	2	3

7.	Body subdivided into 2-4 paragraphs.	1	2	3
8.	Most paragraphs run no more than 5 lines.	1	2	3
9.	Most sentences are 25 words or fewer in length.	1	2	3
10.	Includes complete name and address of letter recipient.	1	2	3
11.	Signed name looks strong and confident using a fountain pen.	1	2	3
12.	Selected a standard type style.	1	2	3
13.	Has a clean, crisp, uncluttered, and professional look.	1	2	3
14.	Used a 1¼" to 1½" margin around the top, bottom and sides.	1	2	3
15.	Confined to a single page.	1	2	3

ORGANIZATION AND CONTENT

16.	Immediately grabs the reader's attention	1	2	3
17.	Presents most important ideas first.	1	2	3
18.	Expressed concisely.	1	2	3
19.	Relates to the reader's interests and needs.	1	2	3
20.	Persuades the reader to take action.	1	2	3
21.	Free of spelling, grammatical, and punctuation errors.	1	2	3
22.	Incorporates the active voice.	1	2	3
23.	Avoids negative words and tones; uses positive language throughout.	1	2	3

24.	Expresses the "unique you."	1	2	3
25.	Employer-centered rather than self-centered.	1	2	3
26.	Stresses benefits the reader is likely to receive from the letter writer.	1	2	3
27.	Demonstrates a clear purpose.	1	2	3
28.	Sentences and paragraphs flow logically.	1	2	3
29.	Includes complete contact information (no P.O. Box numbers).	1	2	3
30.	Expresses enthusiasm, energy, and fire.	1	2	3
31.	Follows the ABC's of good writing.	1	2	3

PRODUCTION QUALITY

32.	Has an overall strong professional appearance sufficient to make an immediate favorable impression.	1	2	3
33.	Used a new or nearly new ribbon (if cloth) with clean keys or printer head.	1	2	3
34.	Adjusted copy setting properly—not too dark, not too light.	1	2	3
35.	Type appears neat, clean, and straight.	1	2	3
36.	Printed with a standard type style and size.	1	2	3
37.	Produced on a letter quality machine.	1	2	3
38.	Proofread and ran "spell-check" (if using a word processing program) for possible spelling/typing errors.	1	2	3
39.	Used good quality paper stock that both looks and feels professional.	1	2	3

40.	Selected a paper color appropriate for my audience.	1	2	3
41.	Compared to nine other business letters received over the past year, this is one of three best in appearance.	1	2	3

DISTRIBUTION

42.	Addressed to a specific name.	1	2	3
43.	Used a No. 10 business or a 9" x 12" envelope.	1	2	3
44.	Checked to make sure all enclosures got enclosed.	1	2	3
45.	Matched the envelope paper stock and color to the stationery.	1	2	3
46.	Typed the address and return address.	1	2	3
47.	Affixed a commemorative stamp.	1	2	3
48.	Used a special delivery service for overnight delivery.	1	2	3
49.	Followed-up letter immediately with a phone call.	1	2	3

FOLLOW-UP ACTIONS

50.	Completed the "Job Search Contract."	1	2	3
51.	Completed my first "Weekly Job Search Performance and Planning Report."	1	2	3
52.	Ended my letter with an action statement indicating I would contact the individual by phone within the next week.	1	2	3

53. Made the first follow-up call at the
    time and date indicated in my letter.   1   2   3

54. Followed-up with additional phone calls
    until I was able to speak directly with
    the person or received the requested
    information.   1   2   3

55. Maintained a positive and professional
    attitude during each follow-up activity.
    Was pleasantly persistent and tactful
    during all follow-up calls. Never indicated
    I was irritated, insulted, or disappointed
    in not having my phone calls returned.   1   2   3

56. Followed-up the follow-up by sending
    a thank-you letter genuinely expressing
    my appreciation for the person's time and
    information.   1   2   3

TOTAL [   ]

Add the numbers you circled to the right of each statement to get a cumulative score. If your score is higher than 60, you need to work on improving your letter effectiveness. Go back and institute the necessary changes to create a dynamite letter.

External Evaluation

You can best conduct an external evaluation of your letters by circulating them to two or more individuals. Choose people whose opinions are objective, frank, and thoughtful. Do not select friends and relatives who usually flatter you with positive comments. Professional acquaintances or people you don't know personally but whom you admire may be good evaluators. An ideal evaluator has experience in hiring people in your area of job interest. In addition to sharing their experience with you, they may refer you to other individuals who would be interested in your qualifications. If you choose such individuals to critique both your letter and resume, ask them for their frank reaction—not what they would politely say to a candidate sending these materials. You want them to role play with you, an interview candidate. Ask your evaluators:

- How would you react to this letter if you received it from a candidate? Does it grab your attention and interest you enough to talk with me?

- If you were writing this letter, what changes would you make? Any additions, deletions, or modifications?

You should receive good cooperation and advice by approaching people for this external evaluation. In addition, you will probably get valuable unsolicited advice on other job search matters, such as job leads, job market information, and employment strategies.

In contrast to the closed and deductive nature of the internal evaluation, the external evaluation should be open-ended and inductive. Let your reader give you as much information as possible on the quality and potential impact of your letter. Taken together, the internal and external evaluations should complement each other and provide you with maximum information.

10

The Letter Sampler: 38 Dynamite Examples

The examples in this chapter follow the principles outlined in previous chapters. They also represent a broad range of letters that should be written for many different types of job search situations. The letters fall into the following job search categories:

1. **Letters to start your job search:** Found on pages 132-137, these letters help get your job search started in the right direction. You write such letters to begin networking and relocation activities, to initiate placement activities, to acquire information on employers, or to get useful job search resources and services.

2. **Letters that lay essential ground work:** Found on pages 138-141, these letters are designed to establish a firm foundation of information, advice, and referrals.

3. **Letters to develop contacts and job leads:** Found on pages 142-144, these are networking letters which are designed for acquiring information, advice, referrals, and vacancy information.

4. **Letters that respond to vacancy announcements:** Found on pages 145-155, these primarily consist of cover letters sent in response to vacancy announcements.

5. **Covers letters that make a difference:** Found on pages 156-159, these consist of four types of cover letters: referral, telephone follow-up, cold turkey, and broadcast.

6. **Resume letters:** Found on pages 160-162, these letters are written in lieu of sending a cover letter and resume. The resume letter merges the two into a single written product.

7. **Follow-Up Letters:** Found on pages 163-165, these critical letters are written at various stages of the job search in response to a variety of situations—requesting information, confirming appointments, inquiring about a job, or following-up a telephone call or interview.

8. **Thank-You Letters:** Found on pages 166-169, these letters should be written for the following job search situations: informational interviews, job interviews, referrals, responding to rejections, withdrawing from consideration, accepting a job offer, and terminating employment.

As you will quickly see, cover letters are only one of several types of job search letters. For more examples of such letters, see the 201 examples included in our *201 Dynamite Job Search Letters* (Impact Publications).

START—Requesting Information
(alumni network)

973 West End
New York, NY 10001

February 13, _____

Wanda Evans, Director
Alumni Services
UNIVERSITY OF
     SOUTHERN CALIFORNIA
1933 Jasper Street
Los Angeles, CA 90312

Dear Ms. Evans:

I've been working in New York City with an investment banking firm since graduating from USC in 1987. I'm now in the process of conducting a job search in the Houston area.

I would like to make more contacts with individuals working in and around Houston. Is there a USC alumni group in Houston or does your office have a listing of USC alumni currently residing there?

I would appreciate any assistance you could give me in making contact with fellow alumni. I'm especially interested in acquiring information on job opportunities in the international investment banking field.

Many thanks for your assistance. I look forward to hearing from you.

Sincerely,

Brenda Carpenter

Brenda Carpenter

START—Requesting Information on Company
(direct contact)

4439 Center Street
Portland, OR 98211

January 30, _____

Melanie Roberts, Director
Public Relations Office
TRC PHARMACEUTICAL COMPANY
1000 West Knight Street
Terre Haute, IN 48732

Dear Ms. Roberts:

I'm in the process of conducting research on various pharmaceutical companies as part of a career development project. Your company was highly recommended as one of the leaders in the field.

Could you please send me information on your company, including an annual report as well as any other information that would help me better understand the future direction of your company? I'm especially interested in learning about your operations in Columbia, Missouri. I enclose a mailing label for your convenience.

Thank you for your assistance.

Sincerely,

Jeffrey Williams

Jeffrey Williams

START—Requesting Information
(relocation)

882 Timberlake Rd.
Minneapolis, MN 54371

February 7, _____

Janice Watson
FIRST CENTURY REAL ESTATE
792 North Adams St.
Suite 319
Knoxville, TN 38921

Dear Ms. Watson:

We plan to move to the Knoxville area within the next six months. Please send us information on your services as well as sample copies of current listings. We would also appreciate any information on Knoxville that would help us better understand the community, such as a directory of churches, schools, and community activities.

We're especially interested in finding a neighborhood with good schools and recreational facilities. We are prepared to look in the price range of $175,000 to $220,000. While we prefer buying, we also would consider renting with an option to buy.

We look forward to working with you in the coming weeks.

Sincerely,

Steven Pollock

Steven Pollock

START—Requesting Information/Registering
(temporary employment services)

1134 Stanford Lane
Orlando, FL 31339

July 11, _____

Janice Eaton
HIGH TEMPS
73 Weston Road
Orlando, FL 31341

Dear Ms. Eaton:

I am interested in a temporary position in word processing. As my enclosed resume indicates, I have over seven years of progressively responsible experience working with a variety of software programs. During the past three years I have extensively used the newest versions of WordPerfect.

Could you please send me information on how I might work with your organization? I assume you have signed contracts with those who register with your firm. Please send me information about your organization as well as the necessary forms for registration.

I would appreciate it if you could keep my resume on file for future reference. Should a position become available for someone with my experience, I would appreciate hearing from you.

I will give you a call next week to answer any questions you might have concerning my interests and background.

Sincerely,

Martin Davis

Martin Davis

START—Contacting Executive Search Firm

1367 River Run Dr.
Burke, VA 23222

September 17, _____

Maryann Philips
EXECUTIVE SEARCH UNLIMITED
821 Shore Drive
Suite 913
Miami, FL 32193

Dear Ms. Philips:

I understand you specialize in recruiting chemical engineers
in the international environmental field. During the past five years
I have worked with the Environmental Protection Agency as a
policy analyst in its Office of International Affairs. I've had a
unique opportunity to apply chemical engineering skills to
important international policy issues.

I plan to leave government for the private sector within the
next 18 months. I'm interested in the possibility of working with
an international contracting and consulting firm in the
environmental field. Since this is an area in which you recruit, I
would appreciate it if you could keep my resume on file for future
reference.

Please let me know if you need any additional information on
my background and availability.

Sincerely,

Debra Follett

Debra Follett

START—Requesting Job Search Assistance

1134 West Ford Ave.
Dallas, TX 73112

August 14, _____

Dr. Delores Clements
DALLAS COMMUNITY COLLEGE
Career Counseling Center
241 Lone Star Blvd.
Dallas, TX 73110

Dear Dr. Clements:

A friend informed me that your Center offers a variety of job search courses and services that are open to the general public.

I've been unemployed during the past three months. So far my efforts at landing a job have not been successful. At this point I think I need some professional guidance to help get my job search on track.

Could you send me information on what types of courses and services you offer? I probably need some testing and assessment work. And I know I could use some assistance on improving my resume.

Sincerely,

Martin Morrison

Martin Morrison

GROUND WORK—Requesting Reference/Contacts
(former employer)

643 Nellum Street
Knoxville, TN 34822

April 9, _____

Susan Jacobson, President
JACOBSON AND TYLER ADVERTISING
239 Wabash Street
Chicago, IL 60003

Dear Susan,

Since leaving Chicago three years ago, I've been working for a small advertising company here in Knoxville—J. C. Thompson. I've very much enjoyed the work. Indeed, I've done some of my most creative work during these past 18 months.

I will be re-entering the job market within the next six months. My present employers have decided to retire after nearly 30 years of business. Since the local economy has negatively impacted advertising, it does not appear the firm will be sold to an outside investor. Consequently, we are all preparing to say "Goodbye." At the same time, I've decided to move to Seattle to be closer to my parents who are now in their mid-80s. I'll be seeking a position in advertising in the Seattle Metro area.

I immediately thought of you as I began planning for this move. I remember how helpful you were in connecting me with my current position for which I am very grateful. Could I again call on you for advice and assistance?

- Do you know anyone in the Seattle-Vancouver area who might be interested in my background?

- Could I use your name as a reference?

I enclose a copy of my resume for your information. Please pass it on to anyone who might be interested in my qualifications.

Will you be attending the National Conference on Media Advertising in San Francisco next month? Marilyn and I will be there for four days, (May 15-18). We'll be staying at the Omni International. It would be great to see you again and perhaps get together for lunch or dinner. Marilyn says she knows some wonderful seafood restaurants you'll just love!

Sincerely,

Bill McDonald

Bill McDonald

GROUND WORK—Requesting Reference
(minister)

7231 Delaware Street
Winston-Salem, NC 39482

March 19, _____

Rev. George C. Allen
CHURCH OF CHRIST
984 Angelical Avenue
Winston-Salem, NC 39482

Dear Rev. Allen:

As you may know, I will be graduating from Central High School in June. In September I will attend the University of North Carolina in Chapel Hill where I plan to major in dental hygiene. Between June and September I'm hoping to land a summer job that will enable me to save money for next year's college expenses.

Would you be so kind as to serve as a personal reference? Since I have very little work experience, potential employers will probably want to know something about my personal character. I thought of you as a reference because I've been very active in our church youth group. I believe you more than anyone else has had a chance to observe me working with others.

I appreciate your assistance. Should an employer ask for a reference, I will give them your name and telephone number.

Sincerely,

Margaret Davis

Margaret Davis

GROUND WORK—Informing About Job Search/
Requesting Advice and Referrals

711 W. End St.
New York, NY 10023

January 4, _____

Darlene Mason
213 Camelback Road
Phoenix, AZ 89241

Dear Darlene,

I just received our alumni bulletin and noticed you now live in Phoenix. What a coincidence. My husband John and I will be moving to Phoenix in April. His company, Sontana Electronics, transferred him to their Phoenix research center.

It will be good to see you again and catch up on the last ten years of our lives. I always remember our late night dorm sessions when we talked at length about what we were going to do when we graduated. Now we should have some really good stories!

I'm sure you could give us some great "Phoenix" tips. One of my major concerns will be looking for a job. During the past five years I have been working part-time as a management trainer. Now that our children are in school, I plan to look for a full-time training position. Should you know of firms that hire for such positions, I would appreciate learning about them. I'm trying to make as many contacts as possible with potential employers before we make the move in April.

We're really looking forward to our move to Phoenix—and seeing you again.

Sincerely,

Margaret Benton

Margaret Benton

**GROUND WORK—Informing About Job Search/
Requesting Advice and Referrals**

203 Jason Drive
Columbia, MO 67332

July 2, _____

Janice Peterson
Guidance Department
JEFFERSON COUNTY HIGH SCHOOL
492 West County Road
Columbia, MO 68221

Dear Ms. Peterson:

It's been nearly four years since I last saw you. I remember how helpful you were when I was trying to decide on my career direction.

As you know, I joined the U.S. Navy immediately after graduation. I've had a chance to learn a great deal during this time, from becoming a communications specialist to having a chance to travel to many parts of Europe and the Middle East. It's been a very interesting and rewarding four years.

I'll be leaving the Navy in another six months. My plans are to return to Columbia and get a job. I'm also hoping to attend junior college on a part-time basis. I eventually want to get my degree in computer science.

I'm really not sure where to start my job search in Columbia. Do you have any suggestions? I enclose a draft of my resume for your reference. Perhaps you know some employers who might be interested in my qualifications. I would appreciate any leads you are able to share with me.

I look forward to seeing you again when I return to Columbia.

Sincerely,

Margaret Snyder

Margaret Snyder

JOB LEADS—Referral
(information and advice)

235 W. Charles St.
Baltimore, MD 21200

July 26, _____

Craig Allen
T. ROWE PRICE ASSOCIATES, INC.
100 East Pratt Street
Baltimore, MD 21202

Dear Mr. Allen:

Jerry Weitz recommended that I contact you about my interests in Graphic Design. He spoke highly of you and said you might be able to give me some useful advice on job opportunities for someone with my background and interests.

Two years ago I completed my Bachelor's degree in Graphic Design. Since then I've been working as a graphic designer at L. C. Printing Company where I've acquired invaluable experience in all phases of graphic design and production. I have a working knowledge of offset printing and have worked extensively with the MacIntosh Computer and QuarkXPress software.

Mr. Weitz said you have been working with one of the country's leading investment firms during the past seven years as a publications oriented graphic designer. I'm interested in learning more about career opportunities with corporations seeking to develop in-house graphic design capabilities. Would it be possible to meet briefly to discuss my career interests? Since my experience has been limited to the printing industry, I'm sure I could learn a great deal from you.

I'll call you on Wednesday afternoon to see if your schedule would permit such a meeting. I really appreciate whatever information and advice you could give me.

Sincerely,

Laura Baker

Laura Baker

JOB LEADS—Cold Turkey
(possible opening)

327 Saffron Court
Pensacola, FL 33218

January 8, _____

Darlene Textron
Editor
HONOLULU STAR BULLETIN
87 Lafayette Square
Honolulu, HI 96829

Dear Mrs. Textron:

For the past two years I have been a copywriter for the <u>Pensacola News-Journal</u>. I have found my time in this position to be both productive and enjoyable. I love writing for the newspaper!

I will be making a permanent move to Honolulu in early April and hope to continue to work in the news department for a major newspaper. I believe the <u>Honolulu Star Bulletin</u> would be a good fit for my interest and skills. As you can see from the resume I enclose, I was graduated from the University of Missouri with a double major in journalism and communication. The combination of my formal training with the excellent experience I have had at the <u>Pensacola News Journal</u> have provided me with a solid background to become a contributing member of another news team. I have been fortunate here to have had the opportunity to work with and learn from some of the best news people in Florida. In fact, I was honored to be awarded the certificate of achievement as best copywriter in Northwest Florida at our regional meeting last month.

I will visit Honolulu early next month to make arrangements for housing and also plan to make contacts with various news organizations. I would like very much to talk with you about possible opportunities with the <u>Honolulu Star Bulletin</u>. I realize that you may not have a position open at present, but I believe it could be in the best interests of both of us to explore possible avenues that might be open in the future.

I will call you next week to see whether we might be able to meet briefly while I am in Honolulu. I will truly appreciate any time you could take from your busy schedule to meet with me. I feel sure I would benefit from having the opportunity to talk with you about the newspaper business in Hawaii.

Sincerely,

Phyllis Jourdan

Phyllis Jourdan

JOB LEADS—Referral
(possible opening)

485 High Bluff Road
Santa Fe, NM 89543

October 3, _____

Rebecca Lyons
WESTERN INDUSTRIES, INC.
98347 W. Main Street
Albuquerque, NM 89977

Dear Mrs. Lyons:

Cynthia Pringle, my current supervisor and an acquaintance of yours, suggested I write to you. I will be relocating to Albuquerque within the next six weeks and will be looking for employment as a secretary. Cynthia indicated your firm is frequently in need of dependable and competent people to fill vacancies.

I have worked for Cynthia for the past three years and have consistently received "outstanding" ratings in all areas on my performance evaluations. I get along well with people and look forward to beginning work in a new firm in my new city.

I will be driving into Albuquerque the week of the 15th and hope I might be able to meet with you at that time. Even if you do not have a vacancy or anticipate one at this time, I would appreciate the opportunity to talk with you about other contacts I might make to further my job search in Albuquerque.

I will call you next week and hope we may be able to schedule a meeting. I will appreciate any assistance you may be able to give me and look forward to meeting you. Cynthia speaks so highly of you that I know your assistance would be truly valuable to me.

Sincerely,

Karen Jostney

Karen Jostney

VACANCY—Director, Business Operations
(Health Care)

STEVEN O'BRIEN

7891 Donner Lane	Orlando, FL 35421	913/371-3981

July 5, _____

Ms. Sharon Campbell
Director, Operations Support
DENVER GENERAL HOSPITAL
2033 Spring Road
Denver, CA 80023

Dear Ms. Campbell:

Your ad in yesterday's <u>Denver Post</u> for a Director of Business Operations attracted my attention for several reasons. I bring to this job

- 8 years of experience in health care finance with a 600+ bed acute care facility
- 5 years of progressively responsible reimbursement experience
- 3 years of management level experience in healthcare billing and collections
- familiarity with major computerized accounting and spreadsheet systems
- a solid record of accomplishment—increased collections by 47% and reduced accounting costs by 36% during the past two years as Assistant Director of Business Operations at Orlando General Hospital

I'm especially interested in moving to Denver where I spent my undergraduate years at the University of Denver. With family there, I already feel part of the community.

I enclose a copy of my resume as well as an article I recently completed on healthcare finance for your reference. The article summarizes much of my philosophy on healthcare finance approaches.

I'll call your office next Thursday afternoon to answer any questions you might have about my candidacy. I also have a few questions about the position.

Sincerely,

Steven O'Brien

Steven O'Brien

VACANCY—Criminal Justice

MARCUS WELLINGTON, Ph.D.

513 Annapolis Road Annapolis, MD 24212   401/238-3192

January 7, _____

Cheryl Grant
Personnel Director
Department of Public Safety
6111 Reisterstown Rd., Suite 110
Baltimore, MD 21222-3142

Dear Ms. Grant:

I read with interest your vacancy announcement in the Sunday edition of
<u>The Baltimore Sun</u> for Director, Division of Parole and Probation. As requested,
I enclose a copy of my resume for your consideration.

I bring to this position nearly 10 years of progressive experience in the
Maryland criminal justice system. After completing my B.A. in Criminal Justice
from the University of Maryland, I worked as a police officer in Baltimore. I
was especially fortunate to work alongside one of the city's leaders in
correctional administration, R. Lance Donovan, who encouraged me to pursue
a Master's degree in public administration with a specialty in correctional
administration.

Since completing my graduate work 8 years ago, I've had a wonderful
career in correctional administration. My work in the fields of parole and
probation have convinced me of the importance of developing new approaches
to correctional administration. During the past three years I've been involved in
developing a model probation program that has reduced recidivism rates by
nearly 30% within a two-year period. I'm excited about the opportunity this
position would afford me to use my experience to further improve Maryland's
parole and probation programs.

I would appreciate an opportunity to meet with you to discuss how my
interests and qualifications can best meet your needs. I'll call your office next
Wednesday to see if we might be able to meet at a mutually convenient time. I
have several ideas I would like to share with you about how I might approach
this position.

Sincerely,

Marcus Wellington

Marcus Wellington

VACANCY—Education

714 W. 42nd St.
Bremerton, WA 98213

October 21, _____

Bruce Davidson
Department of Personnel/
    Human Resources
WALTON MIDDLE SCHOOL DISTRICT
401 McIntire Road
Seattle, WA 98111

Dear Mr. Davidson:

I enclose my resume in response to your announcement in today's <u>Seattle Times</u> for Principal of Walton Middle School. I would bring to this position

- 18 years of progressive experience in education, as both a classroom teacher and administrator

- a demonstrated record of teaching excellence, including teaching awards

- the ability to supervise teachers and classified staff

- a willingness to work closely with parents, teachers, and community leaders

I am currently completing my Ph.D. in educational administration with a specialty in elementary education.

Please let me know if you need any additional information. I will call you next Thursday morning to see if you have any questions about my candidacy. I would appreciate an opportunity to interview for this position.

Sincerely,

Tina Stewart

Tina Stewart

VACANCY—Financial Analyst

ROBIN ANSLER

1061 Wilson Blvd.   Arlington, VA 23122   703/881-8291

January 30, _____

Albert Jones
SPRINT INTERNATIONAL
12220 Sunrise Valley Drive
Reston, VA 22098

Dear Mr. Jones:

I know the importance of maintaining a sound financial analysis in the communication business. That's why I was attracted to your ad in the <u>Washington Times</u> for a Financial Analyst.

During the past four years I've worked in a similar position at MCI. We developed one of the most innovative financial reporting programs in the industry. It helped increase the profitability of MCI's International Voice Products by 22%.

I know your products and services well. Indeed, as MCI's major competitor for offshore customers, Sprint International has an excellent reputation for quality. It's the type of organization I find most attractive for the financial skills I possess. I believe we would work well together.

As indicated in the accompanying resume and in reference to the qualifications outlined in your ad, I have a BA in Accounting and an MBA in Finance. I regularly work with Lotus and Excel and exhibit strong oral and written communication skills.

I'll call your office Tuesday morning to see if you have any questions about my candidacy. I would appreciate an opportunity to discuss with you how my skills and experience can best meet Sprint's needs.

Sincerely,

Robin Ansler

Robin Ansler

VACANCY—Occupational Therapist

717 Georgia Avenue
Indianapolis, IN 48712

March 1, _____

Barry Bates
Human Resources
GREATER INDIANAPOLIS HOSPITAL
67100 Conners Road
Indianapolis, IN 48712

Dear Mr. Bates:

Please consider the enclosed resume an application for the Occupational Therapist position you advertised in today's Indianapolis Journal.

As a recent graduate and licensed therapist, I believe I am well qualified for this entry-level position. Prior to completing my degree and becoming licensed, I worked as a paramedic and volunteer health worker. Facing numerous trauma cases involving auto accidents, I decided I really wanted to work on rehab and acute care cases in a hospital setting. Completing the degree and becoming a licensed therapist is a dream come true.

I would appreciate an opportunity to interview for this position. The acute care unit at Greater Indianapolis General Hospital has a well deserved reputation for excellent patient care. I know since I visited there numerous times with patients. I would be proud to join in contributing to the team effort.

I will call you on Friday morning to see if you have any questions about my candidacy. I look forward to meeting with you and your staff.

Sincerely,

Susan Wright

Susan Wright

VACANCY—Human Resources Analyst

JANET ENGLE
241 Marlboro Lane
Raleigh, NC 27210
717/894-2281

March 11, _____

Gloria Manns
CHARLOTTE-MECKLENBURG SCHOOLS
P.O. Box 30154
Charlotte, NC 28241

Dear Ms. Manns:

Your recent ad in <u>School Administrator</u> for a Human Resources Analyst
interests me for several reasons. I have the necessary qualifications you
outlined for this position. I'm very attracted to the Charlotte area. And I
believe this is a position in which I would excel.

I would bring to this position several important qualifications and
experiences acquired during my 15 years of work in education:

- Master's degree in Psychology
- experience in job evaluation, benefits administration,
  compensation analysis, performance design, and quality
  intervention
- microcomputer proficiency
- knowledge of performance measurement and design models

I would appreciate an opportunity to interview for this position. Please
expect a call from me Thursday afternoon. I have a few questions
concerning this position. Perhaps you also may have questions about
my candidacy.

Sincerely,

Janet Engle

Janet Engle

VACANCY—Information Systems Specialist

231 Westview Terrace
Benton Harbor, MI 48270

February 27, _____

Eric Nelson
NCCR, INC.
1900 North Echos Road
Benton Harbor, MI 48271

Dear Mr. Nelson:

I read with interest your ad in the <u>Benton Harbor</u> times for an Information Systems Specialist. As the accompanying resume indicates, I have the requisite skills and experience you outlined for this position. My 12 years with the U.S. Navy has prepared me well in the use of numerous computer systems and languages.

You may also be interested in several additional skills I would bring to this position:

- designed, coded, and tested network application software
- proficient in several high level computer languages ("C", etc.) and operating systems (UNIX, DOS) and windowing systems (X-Windows)
- planned systems management for communications network
- conducted research and development work on systems management and network simulation

I would appreciate an opportunity to interview for this position. I will call you on Thursday morning to answer any questions you may have concerning my candidacy.

Sincerely,

Dennis Winston

Dennis Winston

VACANCY—Legal Secretary

7172 Whispering Willow Rd.
Columbus, OH 45183

June 4, _____

Thomas Pickering
DIAMOND, ESTER, AND GRACE
718 Jason Avenue
Columbus, OH 45183

Dear Mr. Pickering:

I'm responding to your ad that appeared in Sunday's Columbus Dispatch
for a legal secretary. I have seven years of experience working for a
midsize law firm specializing in patent law. I would bring to this position
the following experience and skills:

- ability to both type and take shorthand at 80+ wpm
- familiarity with Word, WordPerfect, Excel, and Pagemaker
- excellent spelling and grammar skills
- energy, enthusiasm, and the ability to work on my own

I am used to working under deadlines and I am willing to work overtime to
get the job done.

Your ad also mentioned salary requirements. My current salary is $35,500
per year with full benefits. Given my level of experience as well as current
salary ranges for legal secretaries in patent law, I would expect to be
offered this position in the $37,000 to $40,000 range, depending on the
requirements of the job.

Please let me know if you need any additional information. I'll call you on
Tuesday afternoon to answer any questions you may have concerning my
candidacy.

Sincerely,

Margo Redding

Margo Redding

VACANCY—Management/Store Manager

ALICE WALKER
192 West Norton Ave.
Pittsburgh, PA 18291
719/381-9471

January 6, _____

Albert Black
Personnel Department
THE SOUTHLAND CORPORATION
9103 McNeil Street
Philadelphia, PA 17891

Dear Mr. Black:

I read with interest your ad in today's <u>Pittsburgh Times</u> for an experienced Store Manager with good interpersonal skills and three years previous management experience.

As indicated in the accompanying resume, I have the exact skills and experience you require. During the past seven years I have

- managed both a restaurant and retail video store—I know how important good customer relations are to the success of a business!

- supervised up to 12 employees

- made tough hiring and firing decisions

- experienced both the failure and success of two businesses— the restaurant was a victim of arson but the video store was a phenomenal success—increasing annual rentals/sales by 40%

We should talk soon about this position. I'll call you on Friday morning to answer any questions you may have about my candidacy.

Sincerely,

Alice Walker

Alice Walker

VACANCY—Market Analyst

918 Western Blvd.
Kansas City, KS 47831

March 21, _____

Martin Jamison
HEALTHCARE ASSOCIATES
9981 Jefferson Highway
Suite 903
Las Vegas, NV 89312

Dear Mr. Jamison:

I just received this month's issue of Healthcare News and noticed your ad for a Market Analyst with consulting experience.

I believe I have the skills and experience you need. In addition to a Master's Degree in Public Health, I have four years experience as a Market Analyst in the healthcare field. During this time I have conducted over 10 major research projects which involved gathering and analyzing data, writing reports, and presenting findings to funding agencies. I always meet my deadlines and produce first-class products which are well received by sponsors. I am knowledgeable in the use of the two computer programs you mentioned in your ad—WIN 3.1 and EXCEL.

I would be happy to send you a sample of my work, especially a recent report I completed on the comparative costs of alternative healthcare markets for the U.S. Department of Health and Human Services.

I'll call you next Thursday afternoon to answer any questions you may have about my candidacy.

Sincerely,

George Barton

George Barton

VACANCY—Employment Counselor

766 Oro Rio Drive
San Luis Obispo, CA 98734

February 21, _____

Bernard Tompkins, Manager
SUNSHINE TEMPORARY SERVICES
7638 Costa del Sur
Santa Barbara, CA 98763

Dear Mr. Tompkins:

For the past three years I have been an employment counselor with
Solutions for Hire Temporary Services in San Luis Obispo. I like the
opportunity to work with people—both the temporaries and the employers
and enjoy helping them solve their employment problems.

I am responding to your advertisement for an employment counselor that
appeared in today's edition of the Santa Barbara Sun Times. I will be
moving to Santa Barbara in two weeks; I like my work so much that I
would like to remain an employment counselor so your opening looks like
a great opportunity.

I enclose my resume which will give you an overview of my background.
Two of my accomplishments most pertinent to your advertised opening
include:

- Started a new division in our office called "helping hands."
  This division, which provides unskilled workers to factories,
  has proven so successful our company has adopted the program
  in its branch offices nationwide.

- Initiated a temp-employer feedback program that has resulted in
  a 23% increase in business because of greater employer
  satisfaction with the temporary help we provide.

I look forward to meeting with you and having the opportunity to talk with
you further regarding your needs and what I could bring to Sunshine
Temporary Services.

Sincerely,

Jake Weber

Jake Weber

COVER LETTER—Referral

2984 Independent Road
Wichita, KS 58722

April 19, _____

Martha Williamson
MCR VIDEO PRODUCTIONS
8193 Center Street
Wichita, KS 58721

Dear Ms. Williamson:

Michael Thiel recommended that I send you a copy of my resume for your reference. He said he thought you might have an impending vacancy for a Computer Graphic Artist with experience in industrial video production. I have such a background.

I also enclose samples of my work. My background includes strong technical drawing and design skills. I regularly work with an Aurora 240 and MacIntosh. My formal training included work in animation.

Please let me know if you wish to see some of my other work. Since I've worked with Michael on previous video projects, he knows my work well. I'm sure he could answer any questions you may have about my qualifications.

I will call you on Tuesday to answer any questions you may have about my work. Perhaps we could get together to discuss your future graphic art needs.

Sincerely,

Grace Olson

Grace Olson

COVER LETTER—Telephone Follow-Up

781 Lincoln Hwy.
Springfield, IL 62881

May 30, _____

Peter Weston
ALLIED HEALTH CARE
913 West Finley Avenue
Springfield, IL 62876

Dear Mr. Weston:

I very much enjoyed talking with you today about your need for a Senior EDP Auditor. Our conversation got me thinking about both your needs and my future.

I had no idea John Clarkson had suggested me as a possible candidate for this position. While I remember speaking with John recently about my interest in working with a health care organization, I have not been actively pursuing a job change nor seriously contemplating a major move within the near future. However, your phone call got me thinking again about making such a career move.

I enclose a copy of my resume which you requested. I have over 10 years of increasingly responsible accounting experience. During the past five years I have been in charge of the EDP Audit function at Keegan Systems, Inc. I developed and expanded the company's programs, conducted audits of its management information system, and expanded computerized audits. I have experience in auditing large IBM system computers.

Your phone call was the catalyst for rethinking my future here at Keegan Systems, Inc. I would appreciate meeting with you soon to discuss how my interests and experience might best benefit Allied Health care. I'll call you this time—Wednesday afternoon—to see if you are still interested in pursuing my candidacy. In the meantime, I will have a chance to do some more thinking about what I would like to achieve at Allied Health care.

I look forward to meeting you soon.

Sincerely,

Patricia Dooley

Patricia Dooley

COVER LETTER—Cold Turkey

PORTER MACKEL
3891 Terrace Lawn
Jacksonville, FL 35817
319/721-3827

October 3, _____

Martin Shephard
SOUTHERN REALTY
8189 King Street
Jacksonville, FL 35819

Dear Mr. Shephard:

  Whoever said you can't get rich quick never met someone who made their fortune in real estate. While I may not be rich now, I will be soon. And I know I must first have to take some people with me. Those people will also be in real estate.

  I've been a real estate agent for nearly four years. Last year I joined the $2 million club. Next year I plan to be in the $5 million club.

  If you are looking for a top performer who knows how to sell and sell and sell, then we should talk soon. In the meantime, I enclose a copy of my resume for your reference.

  I will call your office on Thursday afternoon to see if your schedule would permit us to meet in the very near future. Since I'm planning to move to another real estate firm within the next two months, I would really like to learn more about your firm and how I might fit into your plans for the future.

        Sincerely,

        Porter Mackel

        Porter Mackel

COVER LETTER—Broadcast

DAVID MARTIN   7713 Montgomery Ave., St. Paul, MN 58219

717/389-9182   Martind@aol.com

July 30, _____

When was the last time you heard an employee say this—*"I'm not performing up to my ability but I promise you will see some major changes within the next three weeks."* I said this last year to my employer.

Three years ago I was so unhappy with my job that I nearly quit. I just didn't have the same level of enthusiasm and drive that I had in previous years. I thought maybe I should start a new career or just take off for a year to figure out what I really wanted to do with the rest of my life. Instead, I decided to rethink how I was doing my present job and perhaps reinvent my chosen career. Expecting to be fired, I went to my boss and told her I was unhappy with my performance. She was surprised at hearing such a confession since she considered me to be above average in comparison to other employees. I told her I could do much better than "above average" and I asked if I could take two weeks off to rethink what I really wanted to do. She agreed and I did my thinking.

It was the best two weeks I ever spent. I decided it was time to do things differently. I sat down and specified two goals I wanted to achieve over the next few years and five related goals to target over the next three months. Then I detailed how I would implement each goal and visualized the final outcomes in terms of percentage increases in productivity.

I returned to work with renewed enthusiasm and drive. Within two months I achieved my three-month goals. I repeated this goal setting and visualizing exercise again and again until it is now automatically embedded into my daily routines.

I am no longer an "above average" employee. I am the top performer. My productivity has increased by more than 50%. I enjoy my work more than ever and look forward to each day with renewed energy.

If you are planning to expand your team to include more self-directed employees, please give me a call. I have more than 10 years of increasingly responsible experience in marketing. I believe I can do for you what I have done for previous employers—take charge and improve profitability. I'll tell you the truth about what I am doing, where I am going, and what I need to do to make my work better than ever.

Let's talk the next time you have a vacancy for someone with my goals and experience.

Sincerely,

David Martin

David Martin

RESUME LETTER—Referral
(Accountant)

443 West Capitol Street
Houston, TX 78261

March 4, _____

Judith Holderman
SIMON AND TUCKER
8813 Tower Avenue, Suite 413
Houston, TX 78269

Dear Ms. Holderman:

While visiting my neighbor yesterday, I met Wendy Watson. After learning I
was in the process of making a job change, she suggested I contact you. She
mentioned you were recruiting for an Accounting/Finance position.

I have more than 10 years of increasingly responsible accounting and finance
experience:

Accountant: Analyzed accounting systems and installed new IBM ledger
system for over 30 corporate accounts. Conducted training programs attended
by more than 500 accountants with small businesses. Developed proposals,
presented demonstration programs, and prepared reports for corporate clients.
Increased new accounts by 42% over a four year period. J.S. Conners & Co.,
Chicago, 1993 to present.

Junior Accountant: Acquired extensive experience in all aspects of corporate
accounting while assigned to the Controller's Office. Prepared detailed
financial records for corporate meetings as well as performed basic
accounting tasks such as journal entries, reconciling discrepancies, and
checking records for accuracy and consistency. Assisted office in converting
to a new computerized accounting system that eliminated the need for
additional personnel and significantly improved the accuracy and
responsiveness. Simon Electrical Co., Chicago, 1988 to 1992.

Accounting Clerk: Acquired working knowledge of basic accounting
functions for a 200+ employee organization with annual revenues of $45
million. Prepared journal vouchers, posted entries, and completed standard
reports. Proposed a backup accounting system that was implemented by the
Senior Accountant. Johnson Supplies, Chicago, 1985 to 1987.

Please let me know if you need any additional information. I will call you on
Thursday afternoon to answer any questions you may have about my interests,
skills, and experience.

Sincerely,

Mary Southern

Mary Southern

RESUME LETTER—Vacancy Announcement
(Bookkeeper)

997 Mountain Road
Denver, CO 80222

June 4, _____

James Fountain
SIMON WALTERS, INC.
771 George Washington Blvd.
Denver, CO 80220

Dear Mr. Fountain:

I read with interest your ad in today's <u>Rocky Mountain Times</u> for a bookkeeper. I believe my experience may be ideally suited for this position:

<u>Manager, Accounts Payable, T.L. Dutton, Denver</u>: Supervised 18 employees who routinely processed 200 invoices a day. Handled vendor inquiries and adjustments. Conducted quarterly accruals and reconciliations. Screened candidates and conducted annual performance evaluations. Reduced the number of billing errors by 30 percent and vendor inquiries by 25% within the first year. 1992 to present.

<u>Supervisor, Accounts Payable, AAA Pest Control, Denver</u>: Supervised 10 employees who processed nearly 140 invoices a day. Audited vendor invoices, authorized payments, and balanced daily disbursements. Introduced automated accounts receivable system for improving the efficiency and accuracy of receivables. 1988 to 1991.

<u>Bookkeeper, Davis Nursery, Ft. Collins</u>: Processed accounts payable and receivable, reconciled accounts, balanced daily disbursements, and managed payroll for a 20-employee organization with annual revenues of $1.8 million. 1984 to 1987.

<u>Bookkeeper, Jamison's Lumber, Ft Collins</u>: Assisted accountant in processing accounts payable and receivable and managing payroll for a 40-employee organization with annual revenues of $3.2 million.

I am currently taking advanced courses in accounting, computer science, and management at Colorado Junior College in Denver.

I will call you on Thursday afternoon to answer any questions you may have concerning my candidacy.

Sincerely,

Jane Barrows

Jane Barrows

RESUME LETTER—Vacancy Announcement
(Sales Manager)

7723 Stevens Avenue
Phoenix, AZ 80023

August 23, _____

Cindy Morrow
HINES DEPARTMENT STORE
1831 Desert Blvd.
Phoenix, AZ 80021

Dear Ms. Morrow:

I am responding to your ad in today's <u>Phoenix Sun</u> for a Sales Manager. I would bring to this position twelve years of progressively responsible experience in all phases of retail sales with major discount stores. I annually improved profitability by 15 percent and consistently rated in the top 10 percent of the workforce. My experience includes

<u>Sales Manager, K-Mart, Memphis, TN</u>: Managed four departments with annual sales of nearly $8 million. Hired, trained, and supervised a culturally diverse workforce of 14 full-time and 6 part-time employees. Reorganized displays, developed new marketing approaches, coordinated customer feedback with buyers in upgrading quality of merchandise, and improved customer service that resulted in 25 percent increase in annual sales. Received "Outstanding" performance evaluation and "Employee of the Year" award. 1991 to present.

<u>Assistant Buyer, Wal-Mart, Memphis, TN</u>: Maintained inventory levels for three departments with annual sales of $5 million. Developed more competitive system of vendor relations that reduced product costs by 5 percent. Incorporated latest product and merchandizing trends into purchasing decisions. Worked closely with department managers in maintaining adequate inventory levels for best-selling items. 1987 to 1990.

<u>Salesperson, Zayres, Knoxville, TN</u>: Responsible for improving sales in four departments with annual sales of $3.5 million. Reorganized displays and instituted new "Ask An Expert" system for improved customer relations. Sales initiatives resulted in a 20 percent increase in annual sales. Cited for "Excellent customer relations" in annual performance evaluation. Worked part-time while completing education. 1984-1986.

Please consider this letter to be my application for this position. I will call you next Friday morning to answer any questions you may have about my candidacy.

Sincerely,

Mark Able

Mark Able

FOLLOW-UP—Vacancy Announcement

997 Mountain Road
Denver, CO 80222

June 11, _____

James Fountain
SIMON WALTERS, INC.
771 George Washington Blvd.
Denver, CO 80220

Dear Mr. Fountain:

I'm not doing well in the telephone department. I called your office several times yesterday but was unable to get through to you. After my sixth try, I decided Thursday was one of your incredibly busy days, and you really didn't need another phone call to top off your day!

I was just following up on my letter of June 4 in application for the bookkeeper position you had advertised in last week's <u>Rocky Mountain Times</u>. Have you had a chance to review my application? I also wanted to let you know that I am still interested in this position and would appreciate an opportunity to meet with you to discuss how my interests, skills, and experience can best contribute to sound financial reporting at Simon Walters, Inc.

I'll try to call you again next Tuesday. Perhaps your schedule will be less hectic by that time.

Sincerely,

Jane Barrows

Jane Barrows

FOLLOW-UP—Vacancy Announcement

712 W. Vermont St.
Washington, DC 20132

May 9, _____

Elliott Stevens
WASHINGTON MONTHLY
1611 Connecticut Ave., NW
Washington, DC 20009

Dear Mr. Stevens:

Just a quick note to clarify my continuing interest in the Summer Circulation Intern position I applied for on May 3. As I discussed with you over the phone today, I was not sure whether I wanted to intern on a part-time or full-time basis this summer. Please don't get me wrong. I don't mean to appear indecisive nor disinterested. I just hadn't thought about the possibility that this would be a full-time position. For some reason I was led to believe, based upon conversations with other classmates who have interned, that most Summer Internship positions were part-time. Now I know better.

After talking with you, I decided to set some priorities in relation to this position and my career interests. What I really want is a full-time position. I think I will both contribute and learn the most by interning on a full-time basis during the next three months.

Will you be scheduling interviews for this position soon? I would appreciate the opportunity to further discuss how my interests and skills could be best used in this position.

Sincerely,

Tracey Nelson

Tracey Nelson

FOLLOW-UP—Vacancy Announcement

717 Georgia Avenue
Indianapolis, IN 48712

March 9, _____

Barry Bates
Human Resources
GREATER INDIANAPOLIS HOSPITAL
67100 Conners Road
Indianapolis, IN 48712

Dear Mr. Bates:

Thanks so much for returning my call today. I appreciated your
thoughtfulness and learned a great deal about your needs and the nature
of the Occupational Therapist position.

As you requested, I instructed my university placement office to send you
a copy of my file. It includes transcripts, three letters of recommendation,
and a sample of my work. Since I requested these documents be sent to
you by Federal Express, they should reach you within two days.

I'll give you a call next week to answer any additional questions you may
have about my interest in this position.

Sincerely,

Susan Wright

Susan Wright

THANK-YOU—Post Informational Interview

4563 Southshore Drive
Key Biscayne, FL 33455

May 5, _____

Marlo Sikes
Public Relations Director
DOLPHIN CRUISE LINE
873 North American Way
Miami, FL 33132

Dear Ms. Sikes:

I am grateful for the opportunity to meet with you today. As Mr. Barnes had indicated, you are certainly one of the best informed persons in the Miami area when it comes to questions about the cruise industry. Your knowledge as well as analysis of future trends is right on the mark, yet I had not looked at it that way before.

My discussion with you helped me focus on the direction I want to pursue. I really believe I would be happier working in a cruise line's corporate offices rather than taking a job on board ship. You mentioned during our discussion that you would be happy to put me in contact with several people in your network if I decided this was the direction I wished to take.

I am writing to ask your assistance in making contact with these people. I will call you in a few days to get these names and addresses from you. I certainly appreciate this additional assistance on your part.

Thank you again for taking time from your busy schedule to meet with me. I look forward to seeing you again in the future—hopefully when I am working for a cruise line!

Sincerely,

Miriam Jordan

Miriam Jordan

THANK-YOU—Post Job Interview

1947 Grace Avenue
Springfield, MA 01281

November 17, _____

James R. Quinn, Director
Personnel Department
DAVIS ENTERPRISES
2290 Cambridge Street
Boston, MA 01181

Dear Mr. Quinn:

Thank you for the opportunity to interview yesterday for the Sales Trainee position. I enjoyed meeting you and learning more about Davis Enterprises. You have a fine staff and a sophisticated approach to marketing.

Your organization appears to be growing in a direction which parallels my interests and career goals. The interview with you and your staff confirmed my initial positive impressions of Davis Enterprises, and I want to reiterate my strong interest in working for you. My prior experience in operating office equipment plus my training in communication would enable me to progress steadily through your training program and become a productive member of your sales team.

Again, thank you for your consideration. If you need any additional information from me, please feel free to call.

Yours truly,

Gail S. Topper

Gail S. Topper

THANK-YOU—Withdrawing From Consideration

2345 Glen Echo Court
Berea, OH 44375

October 7, _____

Dr. Harriet Learner
Chair
Department of Communication
CUYAHOGA COMMUNITY COLLEGE
Cleveland, OH 44452

Dear Dr. Learner:

Thank you for selecting me to interview for the instructor position open in the Communication Department for the coming academic year. I appreciated the opportunity to meet with you and other members of the faculty. You have an outstanding program and it would be a privilege for me to have the opportunity to work with you.

However, I must request that you withdraw my application from further consideration. I have just received an offer from Leeward Community College in Pearl City, Hawaii, to teach in their Department of Speech Communication. This position will give me the chance to further my study of the linguistic components of Native American speech; I hope to be able to complete the book I am writing within the year.

I know you will have no trouble selecting a competent candidate to fill your opening. I do plan to return to Ohio within a year or two to be closer to my parents, and I hope we may be able to get together again at that time. If you have an opening next year in my areas of specialty, I would very much appreciate hearing about it at that time.

I will keep in touch with you over the next year.

Sincerely,

Marcus McDonald

Marcus McDonald

THANK-YOU—Accepting Job Offer

2589 Jason Drive
Ithaca, NY 14850

August 19, _____

Sharon A. Waters
Personnel Director
NEW YORK STATE POLICE
Administrative Division
892 South Park
Albany, NY 11081

Dear Ms. Waters:

I want to thank you and Mr. Gordon for giving me the opportunity to work with the New York State Police. I am very pleased to accept the position as a research and data analyst with your planning unit. The position requires exactly the kind of work I want to do, and I know that I will do a good job for you.

As we discussed, I shall begin work on October 1. In the meantime, I shall complete all the necessary employment forms, obtain the required physical examination, and locate housing. I plan to be in Albany within the next two weeks and would like to deliver the paperwork to you personally. At that time we could handle any remaining items pertaining to my employment. I'll call next week to schedule an appointment with you.

I enjoyed my interviews with you and Mr. Gordon and look forward to beginning my job with the Planning Unit.

Sincerely,

Cheryl Ayers

Cheryl Ayers

cc: Mr. Edward Gordon, Administrator
    Planning Unit

Using Faxes, E-Mail, and the Internet

During the past five years, employers and job seekers have increasingly used faxes, e-mail, and the Internet to communicate with each other. Indeed, many classified ads request job seekers to either fax or e-mail their résumés along with a cover letter or visit the company's Web site for more information. The Web site usually includes information on the company and perhaps a detailed job description with application instructions.

While most of our letter writing principles outlined in previous chapters are valid for these communication mediums, many of our production and distribution principles will differ for faxed and e-mailed letters. For example, while you want to pay particular attention to the color and texture of your stationery when mailing a letter to an employer, these elements may actually work against you when transmitting your letters electronically. Letters on colored paper or heavily textured paper often do not result in clear, crisp copy when faxed. An e-mailed letter with more than 65 characters per line may look poorly formatted.

Faxes

Employers love faxes. It's the preferred distribution method for many employers who seek quick responses to their advertising efforts. If you don't have both outgoing and incoming fax capabilities, you may be at a disadvantage in today's job market. You may have to take your resume and letter to a quick copy center (Kinkos), an office supply company (Staples, Office Depot), or some other service company to have it transmitted.

While faxes are an efficient way of communicating, you should only fax an employer if requested to do so. Unsolicited faxes are not appreciated by most employers. Many employers may request and prefer receiving faxed résumés and letters over mailed or e-mailed résumés and letters; some employers only include fax numbers in their ads. Employers prefer faxes because they are quick and easy to work with in screening candidates. They also neutralize extraneous production and distribution elements, such as paper color and special delivery services, that can influence the screening process.

> **Your fax should look professional and concentrate on your message—why you are especially qualified for the job. Avoid using a computer generated fax program that produces faxes that look like e-mail.**

When faxing a cover letter, make sure your letter follows the writing principles we outlined earlier. It should look professional and concentrate on your message—why you are especially qualified for the job. Make sure you are faxing from a clear black and white original. Avoid using a computer generated fax program that produces faxes that look like e-mail. While such a program may give you inexpensive out-going and in-coming fax capabilities, most of these programs produce unattractive faxes that approximate the look of e-mail. Instead, you should fax a copy of your best paper presentation—complete with all the important formatting and visual design elements we discussed earlier—which you would normally send in the mail to an employer. In fact, if you have the employer's mailing address, your letter can do double duty. Put a copy of the original you faxed in the mail with a note stating that you faxed it on a particular date:

Faxed on July 7

Treat your faxed letter as you would a mailed letter: follow it up with a telephone call. If you can't get through by phone, follow-up with a new fax. However, do not become a pest by refaxing the same information. Employers do remember what they have previously received; they do not appreciate candidates who repeat faxing the same information.

E-Mail

Like faxes, more and more employers request candidates to e-mail their résumés and letters. In fact, many employers request candidates to e-mail their résumés and letters in order to initially screen the electronic "have's" from the electronic "have not's" in today's talent-driven job market. If you don't use e-mail, chances are you will be at a disadvantage in today's job market.

The use of e-mail in your job search will most likely occur in five different situations:

1. Employer requests in a print ad that you apply for the position by e-mailing your resume and letter.

2. You posted your resume on an Internet employment site and employer contacts you by e-mail. You respond by e-mail.

3. You explore job listings on Internet employment sites and respond by e-mailing your resume and letter.

4. You explore company Web pages and respond to job listings that request candidates to e-mail their resumes and letters.

5. You network for job information, advice, and referrals via the Web by contacting relatives, friends, colleagues, former classmates, and teachers or participate in discussion groups that communicate via e-mail.

If much of your job search involves the Internet, most of your communication may take place via e-mail. Make sure you know how to efficiently and effectively handle e-mail, from composing messages and using spell-check to filing them for future reference. Like regular mailed letters and faxes, the most important element in your e-mail will be the message. Your e-mailed letter should follow these basic rules:

1. Organize it like you would a normal job search letter—opening paragraph, body of presentation, and closing. While the medium (e-mail) for your message is different, you still need to communicate an important message. Your message should not be compromised because of the medium. However, you do need to observe

standard rules of e-mail etiquette—no spamming or the use of all caps to emphasize words.

2. Include complete contact information (mailing address, phone and fax numbers, e-mail address) at the end of your letter, immediately following your name.

3. Keep each line to 65 characters or less. If not, your letter may format poorly. Use the "Enter" key to end each line.

4. Be sure to spell-check your letter. Most e-mail programs now have a spell-check function. If not, produce your letter off-line in a word processing program that allows you to spell-check and then clip and paste the composition into your e-mail program.

5. Do not include your résumé as an attachment unless requested to do so by the employers. Most employers prefer seeing your résumé in the body of your e-mail.

If you have the employer's mailing address, do the same as you would do with a faxed letter—send a hard copy in the mail. However, be sure to reformat the letter so it looks very professional. Follow the same production and distribution principles we noted earlier for job search letters. Include a note stating that you e-mailed the letter on a particular date and time.

Faxes Versus E-Mail

If you have a choice between transmitting a letter and/or résumé by fax or e-mail, do so by fax. The reason is simple: most faxed letters, if faxed from an original copy rather than a computerized fax program, look better than an e-mailed letter. A faxed letter maintains its overall professional appearance (format) while e-mail messages may be unattractive when viewed on a computer screen or printed. Many e-mailed letters are poorly formatted and thus do not make a good first impression. At least with a fax of an original letter you can control the print style, highlight various elements, and create an overall professional appearance even though it is being printed at the other end on plain white paper. However, this general rule is quickly changing as more and more e-mail programs have greater capabilities to control formatting elements and produce near letter-quality copy. Within the next two years we expect e-mail to improve to the point where it will be unnecessary to fax résumés and letters; faxes may be considered inefficient dinosaurs!

If an employer gives the option of communicating by fax or e-mail, you may want to do both, as well as put an original copy in the mail, and thereby increase your chances of getting your letter read. We recommend transmitting an attractive letter by fax and immediately following up with a short e-mail message such as this:

> "I faxed you a copy of my résumé and letter at 10:30am today. Please let me know if you did not receive it. I look forward to hearing from you shortly."

You also may want to follow-up by both fax and e-mail within another seven to ten days. We recommend doing this for three major reasons:

1. The e-mail message serves as a form of insurance against fax transmission failure or in case someone else at the other end happened to pick up your fax by mistake.

2. An e-mail follow-up will further help in ensuring you will be remembered by the employer.

3. An e-mail message impresses on the employer that you are technologically literate—you can communicate electronically. Indeed, many employers admit being biased toward individuals who use high-tech communication skills. They feel these individuals are better educated, more intelligent and current, and take greater initiative than applicants who only use the mail or telephone to communicate their qualifications. Communicating by e-mail puts you into a difficult class of job seekers who tend to stand out from the rest.

Major Web Sites

If you're not using the information highway in your job search, you're simply behind the times. You must begin incorporating the Internet into your job search. The Internet is a rich resource for:

1. Acquiring information on employers, the job market, salary ranges, and employer benefits.

2. Networking for information, advice, and referrals.

3. Identifying employment opportunities posted on employment sites, bulletin boards, or company Web sites.

4. Posting résumés in résumé databases which are accessed by employers and headhunters who search for candidates based on keyword searches.

While you may not find your next job on the Internet, you will at least greatly enhance your job search by using the Internet for information, advice, and referrals. The keys to using the Internet are to find the right sites and to communicate effectively by e-mail. For starters, you should visit several of these key employment sites on the Internet:

4Work.com	*www.4work.com*
America's Employers	*www.americasemployers.com*
America's Job Bank	*www.ajb.dni.us*
Best Jobs U.S.A.	*www.bestjobsusa.com*
Black Collegian	*www.black-collegian.com*
CareerBuilder.com	*www.careerbuilder.com*
CareerCast	*www.careercast.com*
CareerCity	*www.careercity.com*
Career.com	*www.career.com*
Career Magazine	*www.careermag.com*
CareerMart	*www.careermart.com*
CareerMosaic	*www.careermosaic.com*
CareerPath	*www.careerpath.com*
CareerMart	*www.careermart.com*
CareerSite	*www.careersite.com*
Careers.wsj.com	*www.careers.wsj.com*
CareerWeb	*www.careerweb.com*
College Central	*www.collegecentral.com*
College Grad Job Hunter	*www.collegegrad.com*
E.span	*www.careermosaic.com*

Headhunter.net	*www.headhunter.net*
Internet Job Locator	*www.joblocator.com/jobs/*
JobDirect	*www.jobdirect.com*
JobTrak	*www.jobtrak.com*
Monster Board	*www.monster.com*
NationJob Network	*www.nationjob.com*
Online Career Center	*www.occ.com*
TOPjobs USA	*www.topjobsusa.com*
Town Online Working	*www.townonline.com/working*
Westech Virtual Job Fair	*www.vjf.com*
World.Hire ONLINE	*www.world.hire.com*

These rich sites will give you plenty of opportunities to communicate your qualifications to employers via e-mail!

Key Electronic Job Search Resources

If you are unfamiliar with how to conduct an electronic job search, including how to best communicate by e-mail, we recommend consulting the following books. These are some of the most useful resources on various dimensions of the electronic job search:

Adams Media, *Adams Electronic Job Search Almanac 1998* (Holbrook, MA: Adams Media, 1998)

Criscito, Pat, *Résumés in Cyberspace* (Hauppauge, NY: Barrons, 1997)

Crispin, Gerry and Mark Mehler, *CareerXroads 1998* (Kendall Park, NJ: MMC Group, 1998)

Dixon, Pam, *Job Searching Online For Dummies* (Foster City, CA: IDG Books, 1998)

Jandt, Fred E. and Mary B. Nemnich, *Cyberspace Résumé Kit* (Indiana- polis, IN: JIST Works, 1997)

Jandt, Fred E. and Mary B. Nemnich, *Using the Internet and the World Wide Web in Your Job Search* (Indianapolis, IN: JIST Works, 1997)

Karl, Shannon and Arthur, ***How to Get Your Dream Job Using the Web*** (Scottsdale, AZ: Coriolis Group Books, 1997)

Kennedy, Joyce Lain, ***Résumés For Dummies*** (Foster City, CA: IDG Books, 1998)

Oakes, Elizabeth H., ***Career Exploration On the Internet*** (Chicago, IL: Ferguson Publishing, 1998)

Riley, Margaret, Frances Roehm, and Steve Oserman, ***The Guide to Internet Job Searching*** (Lincolnwood, IL: NTC Publishing, 1998)

Weddle, Peter, ***Internet Résumés*** (Manassas Park, VA: Impact Publications, 1998)

Write It Right

Whether you conduct a conventional or electronic job search, you still need to write dynamite cover letters and other types of job search letters. Individuals conducting an electronic job search should incorporate the same principles of good letter writing in their e-mail writing. While the medium is different, the message is all the same—you want to communicate to potential employers that you are someone they should invite to a job interview. Your e-mail should be as impressive as your other mail—error free, well organized, and exude competence and enthusiasm. If you can communicate these key qualities to employers, you will be well on the way to landing the job you really want.

The Authors

R onald L. Krannich, Ph.D. and Caryl Rae Krannich, Ph.D., are two of America's leading business and travel writers who have authored more than 40 books. They currently operate Development Concepts Inc., a training, consulting, and publishing firm. A former Peace Corps Volunteer and Fulbright Scholar, Ron received his Ph.D. in Political Science from Northern Illinois University. Caryl received her Ph.D. in Speech Communication from Penn State University.

Ron and Caryl are former university professors, high school teachers, management trainers, and consultants. As trainers and consultants, they have completed numerous projects on management, career development, local government, population planning, and rural development in the United States and abroad.

The Krannichs' business and career work encompasses nearly 30 books they have authored on a variety of subjects: key job search skills, public speaking, government jobs, international careers, nonprofit organizations, and career transitions. Their work represents one of today's most extensive and highly praised collections of career and business writing: *101 Dynamite Answers to Interview Questions, 101 Secrets of Highly Effective Speakers, 201 Dynamite Job Search Letters, The Best Jobs For the 21st Century, Change Your Job Change Your Life, The Complete Guide to International Jobs and Careers,*

178

Discover the Best Jobs For You, Dynamite Cover Letters, Dynamite Résumés, Dynamite Salary Negotiations, Dynamite Tele-Search, The Educator's Guide to Alternative Jobs and Careers, Find a Federal Job Fast, From Air Force Blue to Corporate Gray, From Army Green to Corporate Gray, From Navy Blue to Corporate Gray, Résumés and Job Search Letters For Transitioning Military Personnel, High Impact Résumés and Letters, International Jobs Directory, Interview For Success, Jobs and Careers With Nonprofit Organizations, Jobs For People Who Love Travel, Get a Raise in 7 Days, and *Dynamite Networking For Dynamite Jobs*. Their books are found in most major bookstores, libraries, and career centers as well as on Impact's Web site: *www.impactpublications.com*. Many of their works are available interactively on CD-ROM (*The Ultimate Job Source*).

Ron and Caryl live a double career life. Authors of 13 travel books, the Krannichs continue to pursue their international interests through their innovative and highly acclaimed Impact Guides travel series (*"The Treasures and Pleasures....Best of the Best"*) which currently encompasses separate titles on Italy, France, China, Hong Kong, Thailand, Indonesia, Singapore, Malaysia, India, and Australia. When not found at their home and business in Virginia, they are probably somewhere in Europe, Asia, Africa, the Middle East, the South Pacific, or the Caribbean pursuing one of their major passions—researching and writing about quality arts and antiques.

The Krannichs reside in Northern Virginia. Frequent speakers and seminar leaders, they can be contacted through the publisher or by e-mail:

krannich@impactpublications.com

Index

A

ABCs, 91-92
Action:
    planning, 109-122
    statements, 25
    taking, 86-88, 89-90
Address, 23, 32, 69-70, 83, 103-104
Ads, 17
Advertising, 85-87
Advice, 30, 46-47, 109-110
Age, 19
Aggressiveness, 20, 83
Appointments, 121
Approach letters:
    cold-turkey, 42-44
    example, 53-54
    referral, 39-42
    writing, 38-44
Attention line, 71
Audience, 124

B

Behavior, 3
Benefits, 86
Boasting, 42-43
Body, 72-73
Broadcast letters, 35-38
Broadcasting, 23, 106

C

Closings, 25, 73-74
Cold approaches, 42-44

Communications:
    effectiveness, 11, 64-66
    etiquette, 6
    interpersonal, 6
    mediums, 1
    skills, 4
    written, 6
Competence, 3
Computers, 170-177
Connections, 21
Contact information, 84
Contacts, 21, 45
Content, 38, 82-95, 125-126
Continuation pages, 72-73
Copy reference, 76
Cover letters:
    broadcast, 35-38
    dynamite, 1
    example, 51-52
    importance of, 13-14
    myths, 16-30
    neglecting, 1-2, 22
    purpose of, 21
    targeted 31-35
    with résumés, 23
    writing, 31-38

D

Date line, 68-69
Delivery:
    methods, 104-105
    next day, 28

Design, 64-81
Direct-mail, 35-37
Distribution, 101-108, 127

E
Etiquette, 101-102
Electronic job search, 170-177
E-mail, x, 29, 170, 172-174
Employers:
    communicating with, 2
    contacting, 4-5
    control of, 18
    influencing, 37
    motivating, ix, 2, 9-11, 24
    needs, 6
Enclosures, 76
Envelopes, 29, 102-103
Equipment, 96-98
Errors, 2-3
Ethics, 39, 41
Evaluation:
    conducting, 123-124
    content, 94-95
    distribution, 107-108
    external, 128-129
    follow-up, 121-122
    internal, 123-128
    organization, 94-95
    production, 99-100
    structure, 78-79
Examples:
    cover letter, 156-159
    follow-up, 163-165
    ground work, 138-141
    job leads, 142-144
    letter, x, 10
    résumé, 160-162
    start-up, 132
    thank-you, 166-169
    vacancy, 145-155

F
Faxes, x, 29, 170-171, 173-174
Flattery, 42
Focus, 9, 93-94
Follow-up, 25-26, 29, 42, 106-107,
    109-122, 127-128
Form, 64-81

G
Gatekeepers, 118-119
Gender, 71

Goals, 9, 93-94
Grammar, 83, 90, 97

H
Handwriting, 6, 23-24, 49
Headings, 68
Hidden job market, 34
Hiring, 1
Honesty, 39, 41
Hyphens, 99

I
Identification initials, 75
Implementation, 109-122
Impressions, ix, 13, 65-66
Inclusions, 92-93
Information, 46-47
Informational interviews, 39
Initiative, 25
Ink, 26
Inside address, 69-70
Internet, x, 170, 174-177
Interviews, 4, 15, 39, 45, 116

J
Job:
    changing, 20
    leaving, 48
    market, 17
    offers, 45, 60
    rejection, 45
Job search:
    activities, 3-5
    communications, 14
    competencies, 7-9
    contract, 110-111
    conventional, x
    effectiveness, 7-9
    electronic, x
    letters, 15
    myths, 16-21
    performance report, 112-113
    principles, 16
    process, 3-4
    realities, 16-21
    steps, 3-5
    techniques, 9
Jobs, 17-19
Junk mail, 35-36, 106
Justification, 99

L

Language, 83
Layout, 78
Length, 22, 85
Letters:
    approach, 38-44
    broadcasting, 23
    content, 88-92
    cover, 51-52, 144-159
    distributing, 101-108
    elements in, 66-77
    examples, 11, 130-169
    follow-up, 163-165
    ground work, 138-141
    handwritten, 6, 23-24, 49
    importance of, 13
    job lead, 142-144
    job search, 31-63
    organizing, 82-95
    principles of, 11
    producing, 96-100
    résumé, 50
    role of, 6
    sample, 51-63, 130-169
    starting, 132-137
    thank-you, 44-50, 55-62
    typed, 49
Likability, 18, 34
Luck, 37-38

M

Mailing, 104-105
Margins, 78
Mediums, x
Messages, x
Mistakes, 82-85
Myths, 16-30

N

Names, 26
Networking, 4, 6, 21, 40, 175
Notes, 6

O

Objective, 3
Offers, 45, 47-48, 60
Omissions, 92-93
Openers, 33-34, 43-44, 89
Opportunities, 18
Organization, 82-95, 125-126

P

Paper:
    choices, 99
    color, 27
    quality, 27, 85
    role of, 4
    weight, 28
Paragraphs:
    length of, 22, 72, 89
    spacing between, 99
Pens, 26
Persistence, 120
Personal statements, 40
Plagiarizing, 11
Planning, 87-88
Positive, 91-92
Postage, 28
Postscripts, 76-77
Power, 2, 14
Principles, 11
Printers, 27, 97-98
Process:
    focusing on, x
    job search, 3-4
    letter writing, 11-12
    neglecting, 10
Production, 96-100, 126-127
Professionalism, 6
Proofreading, 97
Punctuation, 83, 90
Purpose, 9, 89

Q

Qualifications, 4

R

Recommendations, 46
References, 24, 93
Referrals, 34-35, 39-40, 52-53, 55
Rejections, 45, 47, 58, 115
Relationships, 46
Remembering, 45, 115, 120
Research, 5
Resources:
    electronic, 174-177
    job search, 13-15
Responses, 36-37
Résumé letters:
    examples, 62-63
    writing, 50

Résumés:
    importance of, 11, 21
    role of, 1
    using, 39, 44

S
Salary:
    history, 24
    information, 93-94
    negotiating, 4, 23
    question, 24
    ranges, 93
Salutation, 32-33, 70-71
Sentence length, 72
Signature, 26-27, 74-75
Skills:
    assessing, 3
    investigative, 4
    job search, 3-5
    writing, 6
Space, 78
Spell-check, 97
Spelling, 83, 90
Stamps, 28
Stationery, 28
Strangers, ix, 2, 6
Structure, 64-81
Style, 77-81, 90-91
Subject line, 71
Success, 20

T
Targeting, 105-106
Telephone:
    follow-up, 35, 42, 116-117
    interview, 41-42
    usage, 40
Termination, 46, 61
Thank-you letters:
    examples, 55-61
    writing, 44-50
Thoughtfulness, 45
Timing, 49
Titles, 70-71
Tone, 83
Type:
    size, 98
    styles, 27, 98
Typing, 23, 50, 77-82, 85, 97
Typewriters, 27

V
Vacancies, 145-155
Value, 3
Voice, 83

W
Web sites (see Internet)
Withdrawal, 47, 60
Women, 32
Word processors, 97-98
Writing skills, 3, 14

Career Resources

Contact Impact Publications for a free annotated listing of career resources or visit their World Wide Web site for a complete listing of career resources: *www.impactpublications.com*

The following career resources, many of which were mentioned in previous chapters, are available directly from Impact Publications. Complete the following form or list the titles, include postage (see formula at the end), enclose payment, and send your order to:

IMPACT PUBLICATIONS
9104-N Manassas Drive
Manassas Park, VA 20111-5211
1-800-361-1055 (orders only)
Tel. 703/361-7300 or Fax 703/335-9486
E-mail: *cover@impactpublications.com*

Orders from individuals must be prepaid by check, moneyorder, Visa, MasterCard, or American Express. We accept telephone and fax orders.

Qty.	TITLES	Price	TOTAL

Job Search Strategies and Tactics

Qty.	TITLES	Price	TOTAL
___	Career Chase	$17.95	___
___	Change Your Job, Change Your Life	17.95	___
___	Complete Idiot's Guide to Getting the Job You Want	24.95	___
___	Complete Job Finder's Guide to the 90's	13.95	___
___	Five Secrets to Finding a Job	12.95	___
___	How to Get Interviews From Classified Job Ads	14.95	___
___	How to Succeed Without a Career Path	13.95	___
___	Me, Myself, and I, Inc	17.95	___

___	New Rites of Passage at $100,000+	29.95	___
___	The Pathfinder	14.00	___
___	What Color Is Your Parachute?	16.95	___
___	Who's Running Your Career	14.95	___

Best Jobs and Employers For the 21st Century

___	50 Coolest Jobs in Sports	15.95	___
___	100 Best Careers For the 21st Century	15.95	___
___	100 Jobs in the Environment	14.95	___
___	100 Jobs in Social Change	14.95	___
___	100 Jobs in Technology	14.95	___
___	Adams Jobs Almanac 1998	15.95	___
___	American Almanac of Jobs and Salaries	20.00	___
___	Best Jobs For the 21st Century	19.95	___
___	Breaking and Entering: Jobs in Film Production	17.95	___
___	Careers Encyclopedia	39.95	___
___	Cool Careers For Dummies	19.99	___
___	Great Jobs Ahead	11.95	___
___	Jobs 1999	15.00	___
___	Jobs Rated Almanac	16.95	___
___	Sunshine Jobs	16.95	___
___	The Top 100	19.95	___

Key Directories

___	American Salaries and Wages Survey	110.00	___
___	Business Phone Book USA 1999	160.00	___
___	Careers Encyclopedia	39.95	___
___	Complete Guide to Occupational Exploration	39.95	___
___	Consultants & Consulting Organizations Directory 1999	605.00	___
___	Dictionary of Occupational Titles	47.95	___
___	Encyclopedia of American Industries 1998	520.00	___
___	Encyclopedia of Associations 1999 (all 3 volumes)	1260.00	___
___	Encyclopedia of Associations 1999 (National only)	490.00	___
___	Encyclopedia of Careers & Vocational Guidance	149.95	___
___	Enhanced Guide For Occupational Exploration	34.95	___
___	Enhanced Occupational Outlook Handbook	34.95	___
___	Job Hunter's Sourcebook	70.00	___
___	National Job Bank 1999	350.00	___
___	National Job Hotline Directory	16.95	___
___	National Trade & Professional Associations 1998	129.00	___
___	Occupational Outlook Handbook, 1998-99	22.95	___
___	O*NET Dictionary of Occupational Titles	49.95	___
___	Professional Careers Sourcebook	99.00	___
___	Specialty Occupational Outlook: Professions	49.95	___
___	Specialty Occupational Outlook: Trade & Technical	49.95	___
___	Vocational Careers Sourcebook	82.00	___

Education Directories

____	Free and Inexpensive Career Materials	19.95 ____
____	Internships 1999	24.95 ____
____	Peterson's Guide to Graduate & Professional Programs	239.95 ____
____	Peterson's Two- and Four-Year Colleges 1999	45.95 ____
____	Scholarships, Fellowships, & Loans 1999	165.00 ____

Electronic Job Search

____	Adams Electronic Job Search Almanac 1998	9.95 ____
____	Career Exploration On the Internet	15.95 ____
____	CareerXroads 1998	22.95 ____
____	Cyberspace Resume Kit	16.95 ____
____	Guide to Internet Job Search	14.95 ____
____	How to Get Your Dream Job Using the Web	29.99 ____
____	Internet Resumes	14.95 ____
____	Job Searching Online For Dummies	24.99 ____
____	Using the Internet and the WWW in Your Job Search	16.95 ____

Best Companies

____	Hidden Job Market 1999	18.95 ____
____	Hoover's Top 2,500 Employers	22.95 ____
____	Job Vault	20.00 ____
____	JobBank Guide to Computer & High-Tech Companies	16.95 ____
____	JobBank Guide to Health Care Companies	16.95 ____

Best Places

____	30 Great Cities to Start Out In	17.95 ____
____	Places Rated Almanac	22.95 ____

$100,000+ Jobs

____	$100,000 Club	25.00 ____
____	$100,000 Resume	16.95 ____
____	100 Winning Resumes For $100,000+ Jobs	24.95 ____
____	201 Winning Cover Letters For $100,000+ Jobs	24.95 ____
____	1500+ KeyWords For $100,000+ Jobs	14.95 ____
____	New Rites of Passage at $100,000+	29.95 ____
____	Six-Figure Consulting	17.95 ____
____	Winning Interviews For $100,000+ Jobs	14.95 ____

Finding Great Jobs

____	5 O'Clock Club Job Search Skills Program	43.95 ____
____	100 Best Careers in Casinos and Casino Hotels	15.95 ____

___	101 Ways to Power Up Your Job Search	12.95 ___
___	110 Biggest Mistakes Job Hunters Make	19.95 ___
___	Adams Executive Recruiters Almanac	16.95 ___
___	Alternative Careers in Secret Operations	19.95 ___
___	Back Door Guide to Short-Term Job Adventures	19.95 ___
___	Careers For College Majors	32.95 ___
___	College Grad Job Hunter	14.95 ___
___	Directory of Executive Recruiters 1999	44.95 ___
___	First Job Hunt Survival Guide	11.95 ___
___	Get Ahead! Stay Ahead!	12.95 ___
___	Get a Job You Love!	19.95 ___
___	Get What You Deserve!	23.00 ___
___	Great Jobs For Liberal Arts Majors	11.95 ___
___	How to Get Interviews From Classified Job Ads	14.95 ___
___	In Transition	12.50 ___
___	Job Hunting Made Easy	12.95 ___
___	Job Search: The Total System	14.95 ___
___	Job Search 101	12.95 ___
___	Job Seekers Guide to Executive Recruiters	34.95 ___
___	Job Search Organizer	12.95 ___
___	Jobs & Careers With Nonprofit Organizations	15.95 ___
___	JobSmart	12.00 ___
___	Knock 'Em Dead	12.95 ___
___	New Relocating Spouse's Guide to Employment	14.95 ___
___	No One Is Unemployable	29.95 ___
___	Non-Profits and Education Job Finder	16.95 ___
___	Perfect Pitch	13.99 ___
___	Professional's Job Finder	18.95 ___
___	Strategic Job Jumping	20.00 ___
___	Top Career Strategies For the Year 2000 & Beyond	12.00 ___
___	What Do I Say Next?	20.00 ___
___	What Employers Really Want.	14.95 ___
___	Work Happy Live Healthy	14.95 ___
___	World Almanac Job Finder's Guide	24.95 ___
___	You Can't Play the Game If You Don't Know the Rules	14.95 ___

Assessment

___	Discover the Best Jobs For You	14.95 ___
___	Discover What You're Best At	12.00 ___
___	Do What You Are	16.95 ___
___	Finding Your Perfect Work	16.95 ___
___	I Could Do Anything If Only I Knew What It Was	19.95 ___
___	Richard Bolles Self-Assessment Tool Kit	19.95 ___

Inspiration & Empowerment

___	100 Ways to Motivate Yourself	15.99 ___
___	Career Busters	10.95 ___
___	Chicken Soup For the Soul Series	75.95 ___

____	Doing Work You Love	14.95	____
____	Emotional Intelligence	13.95	____
____	Personal Job Power	12.95	____
____	Power of Purpose	20.00	____
____	Seven Habits of Highly Effective People	14.00	____
____	Survival Personality	12.00	____
____	To Build the Life You Want, Create the Work You Love	10.95	____
____	Your Signature Path	24.95	____

Resumes

____	100 Winning Resumes For $100,000+ Jobs	24.95	____
____	101 Best Resumes	10.95	____
____	1500+ KeyWords For $100,000+ Jobs	14.95	____
____	$100,000 Resume	16.95	____
____	Adams Resumes Almanac & Disk	19.95	____
____	America's Top Resumes For America's Top Jobs	19.95	____
____	Asher's Bible of Executive Resumes	29.95	____
____	Best Resumes For $75,000+ Executive Jobs	14.95	____
____	Better Resumes in Three Easy Steps	12.95	____
____	Complete Idiot's Guide to Writing the Perfect Resume	16.95	____
____	Designing the Perfect Resume	12.95	____
____	Dynamite Resumes	14.95	____
____	Encyclopedia of Job-Winning Resumes	16.95	____
____	Gallery of Best Resumes	16.95	____
____	Gallery of Best Resumes For Two-Year Degree Grads	14.95	____
____	Heart and Soul Resumes	15.95	____
____	High Impact Resumes & Letters	19.95	____
____	How to Prepare Your Curriculum Vitae	14.95	____
____	Internet Resumes	14.95	____
____	Just Resumes	11.95	____
____	New 90-Minute Resumes	15.95	____
____	New Perfect Resume	12.00	____
____	Portfolio Power	14.95	____
____	Ready-to-Go Resumes	29.95	____
____	Resume Catalog	15.95	____
____	Resume Shortcuts	14.95	____
____	Resumes & Job Search Letters For Transitioning Military Personnel	17.95	____
____	Resumes For Dummies	12.99	____
____	Resumes For Re-Entry	10.95	____
____	Resumes in Cyberspace	14.95	____
____	Resumes That Knock 'Em Dead	14.95	____
____	Sure-Hire Resumes	14.95	____

Cover Letters

| ____ | 175 High-Impact Cover Letters | 10.95 | ____ |
| ____ | 201 Dynamite Job Search Letters | 19.95 | ____ |

___	201 Killer Cover Letters	16.95 ___
___	201 Winning Cover Letters For $100,000+ Jobs	24.95 ___
___	Adams Cover Letter Almanac & Disk	19.95 ___
___	Complete Idiot's Guide to the Perfect Cover Letter	14.95 ___
___	Cover Letters For Dummies	12.99 ___
___	Cover Letters That Knock 'Em Dead	10.95 ___
___	Dynamite Cover Letters	14.95 ___

Networking

___	Dynamite Networking For Dynamite Jobs	15.95 ___
___	Dynamite Telesearch	12.95 ___
___	Great Connections	19.95 ___
___	How to Work a Room	11.99 ___
___	People Power	14.95 ___
___	Power Networking	14.95 ___
___	Power Schmoozing	12.95 ___
___	Power to Get In	24.95 ___

Interview & Communication Skills

___	90-Minute Interview Prep Book	15.95 ___
___	101 Dynamite Answers to Interview Questions	12.95 ___
___	101 Dynamite Questions to Ask At Your Job Interview	14.95 ___
___	101 Great Answers to the Toughest Interview Questions	9.99 ___
___	101 Secrets of Highly Effective Speakers	14.95 ___
___	111 Dynamite Ways to Ace Your Job Interview	13.95 ___
___	Complete Idiot's Guide to the Perfect Job Interview	14.95 ___
___	Complete Q & A Job Interview Book	14.95 ___
___	Interview For Success	15.95 ___
___	Interview Power	12.95 ___
___	Job Interviews For Dummies	12.99 ___
___	Winning Interviews For $100,000+ Jobs	14.95 ___

Salary Negotiations

___	Dynamite Salary Negotiations	15.95 ___
___	Get More Money On Your Next Job	14.95 ___
___	Get a Raise in 7 Days	14.95 ___
___	Negotiate Your Job Offer	14.95 ___

Government & Law Enforcement Jobs

___	Barron's Guide to Law Enforcement Careers	13.95 ___
___	Complete Guide to Public Employment	19.95 ___
___	Directory of Federal Jobs and Employers	21.95 ___
___	Federal Applications That Get Results	23.95 ___
___	Federal Jobs in Law Enforcement	14.95 ___
___	Find a Federal Job Fast!	15.95 ___
___	Government Job Finder	16.95 ___

___ Jobs For Lawyers	14.95	_____
___ Paralegal Career Guide	24.95	_____
___ Post Office Jobs	17.95	_____
___ Quick & Easy Federal Application Kit	49.95	_____

International & Travel

___ Complete Guide to International Jobs & Careers	24.95	_____
___ Great Jobs Abroad	14.95	_____
___ International Jobs Directory	19.95	_____
___ Jobs For People Who Love Travel	15.95	_____
___ Jobs in Paradise	14.95	_____
___ Jobs In Russia & the Newly Independent States	15.95	_____
___ Jobs Worldwide	17.95	_____

Job & Career Series

___ ***"AMERICA'S TOP JOBS" SERIES***	**134.95**	_____
___ ■ 50 Fastest Growing Jobs	14.95	_____
___ ■ Federal Jobs	14.95	_____
___ ■ Top 300 Jobs	18.95	_____
___ ■ Top Jobs For College Graduates	14.95	_____
___ ■ Top Jobs For People Without College	12.95	_____
___ ■ Top Industries	14.95	_____
___ ■ Top Medical and Human Service Jobs	12.95	_____
___ ■ Top Military Jobs	19.95	_____
___ ■ Top Office, Management & Sales Jobs	12.95	_____
___ ***"CAREERS IN..." CAREER GUIDANCE SERIES***	**379.95**	_____
___ ■ Accounting ('97)	17.95	_____
___ ■ Advertising ('96)	17.95	_____
___ ■ Business ('91)	17.95	_____
___ ■ Child Care ('94)	17.95	_____
___ ■ Communications ('94)	17.95	_____
___ ■ Computers ('96)	17.95	_____
___ ■ Education ('97)	17.95	_____
___ ■ Engineering ('93)	17.95	_____
___ ■ Environment ('95)	17.95	_____
___ ■ Finance ('93)	17.95	_____
___ ■ Government ('94)	17.95	_____
___ ■ Health Care ('95)	17.95	_____
___ ■ High Tech ('92)	17.95	_____
___ ■ Horticulture & Botany ('97)	17.95	_____
___ ■ International Business ('96)	17.95	_____
___ ■ Journalism ('95)	17.95	_____
___ ■ Law ('97)	17.95	_____
___ ■ Marketing ('95)	17.95	_____
___ ■ Medicine ('97)	17.95	_____
___ ■ Science ('96)	17.95	_____

___	■ Social & Rehabilitation Services ('94)	17.95 ___
___	■ Travel, Tourism, & Hospitality ('97)	17.95 ___

___	***"CAREERS FOR YOU" SERIES***	**449.95** ___
___	■ Animal Lovers ('91)	14.95 ___
___	■ Bookworms ('95)	14.95 ___
___	■ Car Buffs ('97)	14.95 ___
___	■ Caring People ('95)	14.95 ___
___	■ Computer Buffs ('93)	14.95 ___
___	■ Courageous People ('97)	14.95 ___
___	■ Crafty People ('93)	14.95 ___
___	■ Culture Lovers ('91)	14.95 ___
___	■ Cybersurfers ('97)	14.95 ___
___	■ Environmental Types ('93)	14.95 ___
___	■ Fashion Plates ('96)	14.95 ___
___	■ Film Buffs ('93)	14.95 ___
___	■ Foreign Language Aficionados ('92)	14.95 ___
___	■ Good Samaritans ('91)	14.95 ___
___	■ Gourmets ('93)	14.95 ___
___	■ Health Nuts ('96)	14.95 ___
___	■ High Energy People ('97)	14.95 ___
___	■ History Buffs ('94)	14.95 ___
___	■ Kids at Heart ('94)	14.95 ___
___	■ Music Lovers ('97)	14.95 ___
___	■ Mystery Buffs ('97)	14.95 ___
___	■ Nature Lovers ('92)	14.95 ___
___	■ Night Owl ('95)	14.95 ___
___	■ Numbers Crunchers ('93)	14.95 ___
___	■ Plant Lovers ('95)	14.95 ___
___	■ Self Starters ('97)	14.95 ___
___	■ Shutterbugs ('94)	14.95 ___
___	■ Sports Nuts ('91)	14.95 ___
___	■ Stagestruck ('97)	14.95 ___
___	■ Travel Buffs ('92)	14.95 ___
___	■ Writers ('95)	14.95 ___

	"OPPORTUNITIES IN..." CAREER SERIES	
___	■ Accounting ('96)	14.95 ___
___	■ Acting ('93)	14.95 ___
___	■ Advertising ('95)	14.95 ___
___	■ Aerospace ('95)	14.95 ___
___	■ Airline ('97)	14.95 ___
___	■ Animal & Pet Care ('93)	14.95 ___
___	■ Architecture ('93)	14.95 ___
___	■ Automotive Service ('97)	14.95 ___
___	■ Banking ('93)	14.95 ___
___	■ Beauty Culture ('96)	14.95 ___
___	■ Biological Sciences ('90)	14.95 ___
___	■ Biotechnology ('90)	14.95 ___
___	■ Book Publishing ('87)	14.95 ___

___   ▪ Broadcasting ('92)   14.95 ___
___   ▪ Building Construction Trades ('89)   14.95 ___
___   ▪ Business Communications ('87)   14.95 ___
___   ▪ Business Management ('91)   14.95 ___
___   ▪ Cable Television ('93)   14.95 ___
___   ▪ Carpentry ('93)   14.95 ___
___   ▪ Chemistry ('97)   14.95 ___
___   ▪ Child Care ('95)   14.95 ___
___   ▪ Chiropractic Health ('94)   14.95 ___
___   ▪ Civil Engineering ('96)   14.95 ___
___   ▪ Cleaning Services ('92)   14.95 ___
___   ▪ Commercial Art & Graphic Design ('92)   14.95 ___
___   ▪ Computer Aided Design & Computer
      Aided Manufacturing ('93)   14.95 ___
___   ▪ Computer Maintenance ('95)   14.95 ___
___   ▪ Computer Science ('91)   14.95 ___
___   ▪ Computer Systems ('96)   14.95 ___
___   ▪ Counseling & Development ('97)   14.95 ___
___   ▪ Crafts ('93)   14.95 ___
___   ▪ Culinary Careers ('90)   14.95 ___
___   ▪ Customer Service ('92)   14.95 ___
___   ▪ Data and Word Processing ('96)   14.95 ___
___   ▪ Dental Care ('91)   14.95 ___
___   ▪ Desktop Publishing ('93)   14.95 ___
___   ▪ Direct Marketing ('93)   14.95 ___
___   ▪ Drafting ('93)   14.95 ___
___   ▪ Electrical Trades ('97)   14.95 ___
___   ▪ Electronics Careers ('92)   14.95 ___
___   ▪ Energy ('92)   14.95 ___
___   ▪ Engineering Careers ('95)   14.95 ___
___   ▪ Environmental Careers ('95)   14.95 ___
___   ▪ Eye Care Careers ('94)   14.95 ___

Key Career Kits

___   *"Career Opportunities"* Series   199.95 ___
___   Career Starter Job Kit   139.95 ___
___   Career Software Kit   2199.00 ___
___   City/State Job Source Guides   79.95 ___
___   Complete Career Directories   2369.95 ___
___   Government Job Finding Kit   1189.95 ___
___   Hot Jobs Kit   319.95 ___

CD-ROMs

___   ResumeMaker CD-ROM Deluxe   59.95 ___
___   Self-Assessment CD-ROM Kit   579.00 ___
___   Ultimate Job Source CD-ROM   49.95 ___
___   What Color Is Your Parachute CD-ROM   49.95 ___

Videos

___	60-Minute Self-Renewal Series	999.00	_____
___	Attitude	149.00	_____
___	Interpersonal Communication	249.95	_____
___	JobSearch—Interviewing Success	195.00	_____
___	Job Search: Total Interview	279.00	_____
___	Looking Ahead	129.95	_____
___	Mastering Personal Change!	149.00	_____
___	Power Interviewing Skills	149.00	_____
___	Professional Image Update	579.95	_____
___	Resume Writing Videos	319.95	_____
___	Self-Esteem and Peak Performance	149.95	_____
___	Ten Ways to Get a Great Job	79.95	_____
___	Tough New Labor Market...	195.00	_____
___	Understanding/Using O*NET	119.00	_____
___	Why Should I Hire You?	129.00	_____
___	You're Hired!	129.00	_____

SUBTOTAL _____

Virginia residents add 4½% sales tax _____

POSTAGE/HANDLING ($5 for first
product and 8% of SUBTOTAL over $30) $5.00

8% of SUBTOTAL over $30 -------------------------- _____

TOTAL ENCLOSED --------------------------------- _____

NAME _____

ADDRESS _____

_____

❏ I enclose check/moneyorder for $ _____ made payable to
IMPACT PUBLICATIONS.

❏ Please charge $ _____ to my credit card:
❏ Visa   ❏ MasterCard   ❏ American Express   ❏ Discover

Card # _____

Expiration date: _____/_____ Tel. _____/_____

Signature _____

Your One-Stop Online Superstore

*Hundreds of Terrific Resources Conveniently Available On
the World Wide Web 24-Hours a Day, 365 Days a Year!*

Ever wanted to know what are the newest and best books, directories, newsletters, wall charts, training programs, videos, CD-ROMs, computer software, and kits available to help you land a job, negotiate a higher salary, or start your own business? What about finding a job in Asia or relocating to San Francisco? Are you curious about how to find a job 24-hours a day by using the Internet or what you'll be doing five years from now? Trying to keep up-to-date on the latest career resources but not able to find the latest catalogs, brochures, or newsletters on today's "best of the best" resources?

Welcome to the first virtual career bookstore on the Internet. Now you're only a "click" away with Impact Publication's electronic solution to the resource challenge. Impact Publications, one of the nation's leading publishers and distributors of career resources, offers the most comprehensive "Career Superstore and Warehouse" on the Internet. The bookstore is jam-packed with the latest job and career resources on:

- Alternative jobs and careers
- Self-assessment
- Career planning and job search
- Employers
- Relocation and cities
- Resumes
- Cover Letters
- Dress, image, and etiquette
- Education
- Recruitment
- Military
- Salaries
- Interviewing
- Nonprofits

- Empowerment
- Self-esteem
- Goal setting
- Executive recruiters
- Entrepreneurship
- Government
- Networking
- Electronic job search
- International jobs
- Travel
- Law
- Training and presentations
- Minorities
- Physically challenged

The bookstore also includes sections for ex-offenders and middle schools.

"This is more than just a bookstore offering lots of product," say Drs. Ron and Caryl Krannich, two of the nation's leading career experts and authors and developers of this on-line bookstore. *"We're an important resource center for libraries, corporations, government, educators, trainers, and career counselors who are constantly defining and redefining this dynamic field. Of the thousands of career resources we review each year, we only select the 'best of the best.'"*

Visit this rich site and you'll quickly discover just about everything you ever wanted to know about finding jobs, changing careers, and starting your own business—including many useful resources that are difficult to find in local bookstores and libraries. The site also includes tips for job search success and monthly specials. Its shopping cart and special search feature make this one of the most convenient Web sites to use. Impact's Internet address is:

www.impactpublications.com